Evaluating Accessibility
in Museums

Evaluating Accessibility in Museums

A Practical Guide

Edited by Laureen Trainer

ROWMAN & LITTLEFIELD
Lanham • Boulder • New York • London

Published by Rowman & Littlefield
An imprint of The Rowman & Littlefield Publishing Group, Inc.
4501 Forbes Boulevard, Suite 200, Lanham, Maryland 20706
www.rowman.com

86-90 Paul Street, London EC2A 4NE

British Library Cataloguing in Publication Information Available

Library of Congress Cataloging-in-Publication Data
Names: Trainer, Laureen, editor.
Title: Evaluating accessibility in museums : a practical guide / edited by Laureen
    Trainer.
Description: Lanham : Rowman & Littlefield, [2024] | Includes bibliographical
    references and index.
Identifiers: LCCN 2024005938 (print) | LCCN 2024005939 (ebook) | ISBN
    9781538186305 (cloth) | ISBN 9781538186312 (paperback) | ISBN 9781538186329
    (ebook)
Subjects: LCSH: Museums and people with disabilities—United States. | Museum
    techniques—Evaluation—United States. | Museum buildings—Barrier-free design—
    United States.
Classification: LCC AM160 .E83 2024 (print) | LCC AM160 (ebook) | DDC
    069/.170973—dc23/eng/20240317
LC record available at https://lccn.loc.gov/2024005938
LC ebook record available at https://lccn.loc.gov/2024005939

Contents

Contents

Preface

WHY ACCESSIBILITY AND EVALUATION?

Laureen Trainer

The idea for this book came when I was curating a blog series for the Committee on Audience Research and Evaluation (CARE), a former professional network of the American Alliance of Museums (AAM). In that role, I was always searching for evaluation topics that would be of interest to the wider field, and in the fall of 2022, I decided I wanted to dig deeper into accessibility. As it happened, two colleagues in Denver, Heather Pressman and Danielle Schulz, had recently published a book on the topic, *The Art of Access: A Practical Guide for Museum Accessibility*,[1] so I reached out to ask them to write something. I knew from their work that they would provide invaluable information and examples of how to identify and remove barriers to access. But since this was for CARE, we also needed to focus on the role of evaluation in that process. Casting a wide net led me to three institutions that were using evaluation to fuel their accessibility initiatives: the Intrepid Museum, the Nelson-Atkins Museum of Art, and the Henry Ford. Staff from all three museums agreed to share their experiences in the post, following an informative introduction from Pressman and Schulz. The resulting post, "Museum Accessibility: An Art and a Science," went live on October 21, 2022,[2] and just six weeks later it was named the fourth-most-read AAM blog post of the year![3]

That's when I realized we were onto something bigger—that we had tapped into an emerging area of evaluation that could help museums reimagine their impact and understand how to better serve more visitors. To explore that potential further, I began to think about how we could expand the piece into an edited book. I started to search for additional authors who could participate, leading me to numerous wonderful conversations with museum professionals doing innovative work to enable all people to participate equitably in museums. It became clear that an emphasis on access, while too long coming in many instances, had now arrived in the field, with a growing number of institutions focusing on how to welcome visitors from disability communities.[4] Museums were beginning to realize that access lies at the heart of diversity, equity, and inclusion, and that it is impossible to realize any of those values without it. Access is what allows you to welcome a neurologically, physically, and developmentally diverse community; create accommodations that allow for equitable involvement; and provide inclusive experiences that benefit everyone. I became more confident than ever that the time was right for a book that shared strategies for purposeful, data-led initiatives in the area.

WHY ACCESSIBILITY?

There are more than one billion disabled people on the planet, and in the United States alone, the Centers for Disease Control and Prevention estimate that one in four adults have a disability[5] and one in six children have a developmental disability.[6] These numbers, unlike many other demographics, change daily, as people can move in and out of disability over the course of their lives, such as when they experience injury or disease, like long COVID, as a recent example.[7] Disabilities can be permanent, temporary, or situational. They can be congenital or acquired. (Most likely, all of us will acquire a disability of some kind as we age.) Some disabilities are visible, but most are not. People can have more than one disability. Disabilities are one part of people's identities but intersect with others.

In other words, people with disabilities are a significant part of your community, no matter where you are and what type of institution you're affiliated with. The scope of people impacted by accessibility concerns grows even larger when you consider that most people visit your institution in a group—whether as an adult-only group or as a family group[8]—and that groups are motivated by the prospect of social interaction with one another. Being able to move through a space, engage in interactives, and learn together is an important part of the group dynamic. Therefore, if barriers exist that impede even one person, everyone with them will likely not feel welcome either. As the authors of a recent study on belonging from the Science Museum of Minnesota put it, "Belonging is felt not just on an individual level but as a group. Where an individual in a visiting group is not supported—perhaps their identity is not represented, or their access to an exhibit is impeded—the impact is felt by the unsupported individual *and* the group as a whole."[9]

To experience unified belonging, this expansive audience would benefit from accommodations that reduce barriers that lead to frustration and isolation in our institutions. These can include environmental barriers, such as difficulties with physical entry, mobility, wayfinding, or sensory stimulation; communication barriers, such as onerous accommodation request processes or negative interactions with untrained staff; collections barriers, such as difficulties viewing objects behind glass or under low lighting for protection; and social barriers, such as the inability to fully participate as a group without relying on nondisabled members for support.[10] At its heart, creating an accessible environment means engaging with disability communities and recognizing them as

Laureen Trainer

experts and co-creators. It is about understanding what makes an environment or experience appealing to all, easy for all to comprehend and use, and possible for all to move around and interact with in similar fashions. If museums wish to be considered essential community assets with resources open to all, this is indispensable work. You can't be essential to all without being accessible to all.

You may have come across the phrase "nothing about us without us," which came into use in disability activism during the 1990s.[11] The slogan communicates a fundamental truth about accessibility work: that you should not undertake policies, actions, and programs that affect disabled visitors without the active involvement of disabled people themselves. Otherwise, you risk creating policies and actions that are ill-informed, ineffective, or even harmful. The core principles of the slogan—inclusive, participatory, empowering—provide a road map for museums in thinking about their relationship to disability communities:

1. Inclusive: Museums should seek out and meaningfully engage with the voices, perspectives, and experiences of disabled individuals and disability communities as they create exhibitions, programs, and policies.
2. Participatory: Museums should invite disabled individuals and disability communities to share their desires, needs, and challenges to inform policies, programs, and exhibitions, with the understanding that multiple methods may be necessary at any one time, and that different communities have differing and perhaps conflicting needs.
3. Empowering: Museums should welcome the distinctive perceptions and perspectives disabled individuals and disability communities bring, which can offer new ideas that may ultimately benefit many other groups.

As you read through the chapters in this book, you will find that each of the initiatives they describe share these principles in common. Every author engaged with disability communities to develop and iterate programming and exhibition ideas, and to design and refine prototypes. This level of inclusivity, participation, and empowerment improved the final products for disabled and nondisabled visitors alike and strengthened relationships between the institutions and their communities. When museum staff and disabled community members engage in the design process as a team of learners and experts, they improve the museum experience for everyone, create opportunities for reflection and growth, and push institutions to think and act in new and revolutionary ways.

WHY EVALUATION?

As I pursued my mission to find additional authors for this book, I learned of many innovative and important accessibility initiatives, programs, and exhibitions taking place in museums. What was harder to find were institutions doing this work *and* evaluating it—which I believe is to the detriment of the field. Without evaluating your initiatives, whether accessibility related or not, you are cut off from understanding their impact. You miss information on what you are doing well and where you are making mistakes, making it more difficult to iterate and improve. Furthermore, you miss a crucial chance to connect with the community you aim to serve, as evaluating your programs necessitates engaging with the members of that community.

Evaluation serves many purposes, but at its core it is about assessing and judging the quality and effectiveness of something—whether an idea, a program, a label, an interactive, an exhibition, or a policy. It is about understanding the impact of your work on different internal and external communities. It is about documenting thoughts and processes for you and others to learn from. It is about knowing whether you were successful—however you defined success. It is about gathering data for making current and future decisions. And it is about bringing different voices into your conversations and decisions. Here are some common purposes of evaluation that may have a place in helping you understand your accessibility programs and initiatives:

1. Needs assessment: Determining the current status of something and then identifying and naming the gaps between that current state and a preferred future state.
2. Improvement: Shedding light on ways to enhance quality and effectiveness, often through continuous improvement.
3. Learning and knowledge building: Discovering answers to questions and analyzing what worked and what didn't work, as well as unintended outcomes.
4. Communication: Relaying your impact and the value of your programs, exhibitions, and policies to internal and external stakeholders.
5. Accountability: Understanding whether what you thought was going to happen did happen.
6. Decision making: Providing context that can inform decision making, often by bringing outside voices, thoughts, and ideas into internal processes.

The chapters in this book touch on every one of these purposes. They also address many different types and tools of evaluation, meaning that depending on where you and your institution are along your evaluation journey, you may encounter some terms that are new to you. To ease your learning process, I've defined some of those terms below, organizing them in two broad categories: stages of evaluation and methodology.

STAGES OF EVALUATION[12]

1. Front end: Takes place at the beginning of an idea or project to help guide thinking and concepts. Provides information for future planning; can reveal visitors' prior knowledge, experience, and expectations.

Laureen Trainer

2. Formative or prototyping: Takes place in the development process of an idea or project. Examines how well something (e.g., a program, exhibit component, interactive, label) is working, where people are stumbling, where glitches and bottlenecks are occurring, and how people are responding to the content, design, and functionality, so that improvements can be made before the program is delivered or the exhibition opens.
3. Remedial: Takes place immediately after a project debuts (e.g., a program is given for the first time or an exhibition opens). Serves to identify problems or weaknesses so that they can be addressed immediately. After these issues are rectified, the summative evaluation phase can proceed.
4. Summative: Takes place after the execution of a project. Gathers data on the impact of the program or exhibition to understand visitor learning, attitudes, and behavior with an eye toward future improvement and iterations.

METHODOLOGIES[13]

1. Survey: A set of questions, typically self-administered by the respondent with pen and paper or on a tablet or computer, and containing more quantitative (i.e., numerical and measurable) than qualitative (i.e., open-ended, descriptive, and interpretive) prompts. Surveys can reach a broad audience, but with limited depth as there is no opportunity for follow-up. They can be administered before and/or after a program. For documenting change over time, they can be administered *both* before and after (pre-post surveys), or as a retrospective pre-post survey (asking respondents to reflect back on how they felt about something before an experience and how they feel at the time of the survey).
2. Interviews: A set of questions asked by an interviewer to an interviewee in a conversational manner. Interviews can provide a wealth of information, as they allow the time and space to develop thoughts and offer clarification. This enables them to get to the "how" and "why" of an issue, whereas surveys are best at getting to the "what." Interviews can be structured (i.e., using an established "protocol" with key questions that allows for little deviation or probing), semistructured (i.e., a general set of questions with flexibility for the interviewer to ask additional questions in the moment or choose not to ask every question), or unstructured (i.e., a freeform conversation without predefined questions).
3. Focus groups: Groups of people assembled based on similar characteristics or interests to offer their thoughts and ideas on a topic. As with interviews, facilitators usually come to focus groups prepared with general questions to help guide the conversation, but it is the group dynamic and the ability to hear from others—potentially sparking new ideas and viewpoints—that provides the richness of insight.

4. Observations: Systematically watching people in an exhibition, program, or other museum feature to uncover common behaviors and trends. Evaluators may create a checklist of behaviors to observe ahead of time, watch several people and begin to identify trends and interactions as they emerge, or a combination of both approaches. Another methodology called timing and tracking falls under observation and is generally used to understand how long people spend in exhibitions, where they go, and what they engage with.
5. Secondary research: Using the findings from other research and evaluation studies to inform and guide your own programs, exhibits, and policies.

HOW IS THIS DIFFERENT FROM OTHER BOOKS?

There are books on museum accessibility and books on museum evaluation, but none before this one on the intersection between the two.[14] Books on museum accessibility typically focus only on the need for accessibility and how to begin implementing accessibility initiatives. Books on museum evaluation tend to concentrate exclusively on the importance of evaluation and how to launch evaluation initiatives. While both perspectives are essential, thinking and reading about them separately can lead to siloed discussions and actions. Bridging the two fields can create more welcoming, inclusive, accessible, equitable, and diverse institutions—ones that better reflect, engage, and empower the spectrum of our communities.

This book combines these two worlds through case studies that highlight the impact of evaluation in accessibility work. I hope it inspires institutions who have yet to start thinking about accessibility to begin those conversations, those already doing accessibility work to continue their learning journey by engaging in evaluation, and those already evaluating their initiatives to consider new ideas and approaches. This book is both for those who are knee-deep in creating accessible programs, exhibits, and policies and for those who are still contemplating what the first step on their accessibility journey might look like. It is also for those in the museum field who focus on evaluation work and audience research and for those just beginning to ask questions about evaluation. Each chapter provides examples of programs and accommodations for disabled visitors, considerations that go into creating accessible exhibit components and exhibitions, new thinking about how to welcome and engage disabled visitors, and recommendations for the field. The chapters also detail evaluation questions, methodologies, findings, and data-informed decisions, as well as provide information related to staff training, the formation of accessibility advisory groups, and lessons learned.

The case studies in this book come from institutions of various sizes (small, medium, and large), types (art, science, history, zoo, children's museum, and aquarium), and geographical locations (Massachusetts, New York, Texas, California, Washington, and Missouri) to highlight how a range of different organizations have developed and grown accessibility initiatives and the vital role that evaluation has played in their evolution. In each chapter, you will learn about various types of accessibility initiatives *and* how they have been evaluated, the impact of these programs on disabled (and at times, nondisabled) visitors, and what staff and community members learned. In each case, the combination of accessibility and evaluation created more responsive institutions who value, and are in dialogue with, their communities.

WHAT YOU'LL FIND IN THE COMING CHAPTERS

Chapter 1: The Art of Accessible Evaluation by Heather Pressman and Danielle Schulz
Keywords: museum accessibility, DEAI, accessible evaluation, disability representation

The authors of *The Art of Access: A Practical Guide for Museum Accessibility*, Pressman and Schulz, provide an introduction to museum accessibility and set the stage for the following chapters. They emphasize the importance of making museums accessible to people with disabilities, pointing out that it is not only a legal requirement but also a fundamental aspect of museums' missions to ensure that learning opportunities are available to everyone in the community. They share information about accessibility as it relates to the law and as it relates to serving all your visitors (including numerous ways museums can work to break down barriers to access), stress the importance of including diverse voices in all planning for exhibitions and programs, and detail numerous ways in which museums can work to become more accessible. They then introduce the concepts of accessible evaluation—using practices and methodologies that work for people with disabilities—and evaluating accessibility—collecting feedback that allows you to understand your impact on disability communities and increase your learning. They highlight examples and identify opportunities and pitfalls throughout the chapter.

Chapter 2: Centering First-Person Perspectives in an Exhibit Accessibility Audit by Sarah Brenkert, Malikai Bass, Dillyn Adamo, and Ellie Kravets
Keywords: ableism, models of disability, museology

Brenkert and colleagues share a story of a "standard" front-end evaluation that proved to be anything but. At its heart, this chapter represents an awakening to the full meaning of accessibility, sharing important philosophical insights the authors picked up in the process. As the Seattle Aquarium worked with three evaluation students from the University of Washington's museology program—all of whom who identified as disabled, a disability activist, or both—

staff came to realize the ableist mindsets that infused their evaluation thinking. For example, in treating "general visitors" as an undifferentiated aggregate, they presumed that disabled visitors have experiences that do not differ from majority experiences in any important ways. This chapter follows the staff's journey as they reflected on ableism in evaluation, learned about models of disability, and listened to the lived experiences of the student evaluators. The authors also document their evaluation questions, detail the methods used in their accessibility audit, and share results and recommendations for change.

Chapter 3: Access from the Ground Up: Designing a Museum Facility with Access in Mind by Lisa Eriksen, Tina Keegan and Maia Werner-Avidon
Keywords: zoo, children's museum, exhibition design

The Palo Alto Junior Museum & Zoo's accessibility and inclusion story starts at the very beginning—with staff realizing that they wanted to engage service providers and parents of children with disabilities in conversation—and concludes with a multilayered initiative that transformed the institution as a whole. In 2010, the museum took its first steps to learn how it could make its exhibits more accessible. When just one year later the organization embarked on a master planning and capital campaign to replace its aging, eighty-plus-year-old facility, staff recognized a unique opportunity to design for accessibility from the ground up. An IMLS grant provided funding for a project to address the lack of quality science learning experiences for children with disabilities and their families by creating an accessibility advisory team, providing staff training, and developing exhibits and access resources for the new museum and zoo.

The authors share how members of disability communities provided feedback on everything from architectural and design plans to exhibit elements and resources, such as tactile maps or sensory backpacks for use by children on the autism spectrum. They then detail aspects of the summative evaluation and share results that show the impact on families both with and without disabilities, demonstrating that accommodations created for one group often benefit all visitors.

Chapter 4: Making History Accessible: Evaluation and Stakeholder Involvement in the Evolution of an Access Initiative by Charlotte J. Martin and Lynda Kennedy
Keywords: historic houses and sites, historic preservation, user testing, multi-sensory interpretation

This chapter follows staff as they tackle physical and sensory barriers at a museum centered on a landmarked aircraft carrier that served in the US Navy from 1943 to 1974, with collections including a submarine and the supersonic commercial airliner Concorde. Given the historic preservation constraints of its site, the Intrepid Museum does not immediately come to mind as an accessible space, but Martin and Kennedy share how it nonetheless became a leader in the museum accessibility field, as staff started with their strengths and grew stronger through evaluation. Staff used evaluation to engage with stakeholders, learn more about the needs of disability communities, understand what works and doesn't for different disability communities, prototype and adapt ideas, measure success, and inform future improvements. Throughout the chapter, the authors share program ideas, evaluation methods, and recommendations for the field.

They then report on an IMLS-funded grant project where the museum partnered with New York University's Ability Project. The project paired students with staff at multiple historic sites to develop prototypes responding to the needs of each specific site and its visitors with disabilities. User testing and other evaluation methods were a key part of the prototyping process and even informed the writing of a resulting digital toolkit, *Making History Accessible: A Toolkit for Multisensory Interpretation*, which is available on the museum's website.

Chapter 5: Integrating Formative Accessibility Testing into Evaluation for an Immersive STEM Exhibition by Elizabeth Kunz Kollmann, Leigh Ann Mesiti Caulfield, and Tim Porter
Keywords: formative evaluation, universal design, universal design for learning, accessibility testing, exhibition

In this chapter, staff from the Museum of Science, Boston, detail the large-scale formative evaluation of *Arctic Adventure: Exploring with Technology*, an immersive physical and digital exhibition with several cognitive and sensory components that required rigorous testing to ensure they were accessible to all visitors. The museum has a long and rich history of evaluation, but this project required that everyone involved—project managers, content developers, exhibit designers, internal evaluators, and an external partner—embrace experimentation and iterative approaches in a whole new way.

Throughout the project, the team employed several evaluation methods to answer usability questions, understand patterns of use, and refine interactive components so that *Arctic Adventure* would be accessible to the greatest number of visitors, including those with a range of disabilities. They began by utilizing personas to think about the experience that visitors with disabilities might have at different components within the exhibition and then moved on to extensive rounds of user testing on experiential components. Members of the museum's exhibit accessibility testing database and their external Accessibility Advisory Committee participated in several rounds of prototyping, shaping numerous changes to the final exhibition that Kollman, Caulfield, and Porter document in the chapter. They also share lessons learned from the experience, such as the importance of early prototyping, as well as a few places where an interactive fell short of being accessible to all even after this extensive testing.

Chapter 6: An Iterative Approach to Accessibility: Transforming Museum Process with Experimentation and Evaluation by Sarah Schleuning
Keywords: sensory processing, cognitive accessibility, exhibition design

In this chapter, Schleuning tells the story of curating, designing, and evaluating *speechless: different by design* at the Dallas Art Museum, an exhibition that challenged the standard way of experiencing museum content: looking at an object and reading labels. *speechless* explored the range of ways we process sensory information and sought to develop an expanded appreciation and empathy for how people with neurological differences experience the world and how the world responds to them. Azucena Verdín, the exhibition's evaluator, reviewed scientific literature to explore how indicators of human sensory phenomena, including individual sensitivities, thresholds, and preferences, could be measured reliably and devised a way to document the varied responses visitors may have as they interacted with art through touch, sound, sight, and vestibular and proprioceptive input. Schleuning and Verdín also explored whether and how social experiences were influenced by differences in sensory sensitivities.

Chapter 7: Beyond Participant Data: Alternative Ways of Measuring Impact by Karen Breece, Kelsey Van Voorst, and Maia Swinson
Keywords: ethics, dementia, aging populations, secondary research

Conner Prairie is a historic site and interdisciplinary museum focusing on historic trades, livestock, nature, civics, live interpretation, and education for all ages. Looking to expand programming to the aging population in their local communities, educators realized that Memory Cafés (social gatherings for those with memory loss and their caregivers) would serve their intended audience and utilize all aspects of the site. They turned to research about dementia, Alzheimer's, and the needs of caregivers to inform the creation of their Memory Café programs. However, as they began to think about evaluating these new programs, they realized that traditional methods such as surveys and interviews were not appropriate for this vulnerable population, and perhaps even unethical, as a person's cognitive disability may compromise their capacity to make a reasoned decision about participating in the evaluation study.[15]

This chapter highlights that not all programs need first-person data collection to evaluate success and understand impact. The authors present considerations for evaluating the experiences of people with dementia, many of which can be applied to other visitors who may have visible or invisible differences or disabilities. They share the methods they used to evaluate their program,

Laureen Trainer

which relied heavily on secondary research and evaluation studies. They also provide guidance for conducting a literature review, which is a crucial method for identifying and documenting relevant secondary research.

Chapter 8: The Deaf Culture Project: Setting an Expectation of Adaptability by Alyssa Carr
Keywords: d/Deaf, hard of hearing, culture, adaptability, culturally responsive participatory evaluation

The last case study in the book is at once the narrowest and the most expansive, as it focuses on one museum's outreach to one particular disability community, yet reveals the nuances of identity and experience that emerge as we move beyond broad, generic accessibility initiatives. The Nelson-Atkins Museum of Art began working with organizations serving the d/Deaf and hard-of-hearing community in 2015, forming several consistent and established partnerships in the ensuing years. Therefore, when staff received a three-year grant from the Institute of Museum and Library Services (IMLS) for the Deaf Culture Project, they thought they had laid ample groundwork to form a successful initiative. However, they soon realized that there was still much more to learn about and from the d/Deaf and hard-of-hearing community to create accessible programming for their partners and visitors. This chapter details how evaluation led to an expectation of adaptability, as almost every part of the grant changed—for the better—over the three-year cycle. Carr also shares information about staff training, notes lesson learned, and provides general recommendations for working with the d/Deaf and hard-of-hearing community.

Each of the case studies reveals how these institutions used evaluation to refine and enhance their programs and exhibits, while also demonstrating the importance of always talking, always asking, always adapting, and always using evaluation to help guide you forward. This work is a process; it is iterative and ongoing. Let's get started!

NOTES

1. Heather Pressman and Danielle Schulz, *The Art of Access: A Practical Guide for Museum Accessibility* (Lanham, MD, Rowman & Littlefield, 2021).
2. *"Museum Accessibility: An Art and a Science."* American Alliance of Museums, accessed November 29, 2023. https://www.aam-us.org/2022/10/21/museum-accessibility-an-art-and-a-science/
3. "The Top Ten Alliance Blog Posts of 2022." American Alliance of Museums, accessed November 29, 2023. https://www.aam-us.org/2022/12/23/the-top-ten-alliance-blog-posts-of-2022/?utm_source=American+Alliance+of+Museums&utm_campaign=030b8e0384-FieldNotes_2022_Dec26&utm_medium=email&utm_term=0_-030b8e0384-%5BLIST_EMAIL_ID%5D

4. A note about language. I use identity-first language throughout this chapter, while most of the authors use person-first language in their writings. I thought the juxtaposition of the two styles would be helpful for readers to see. Neither of these choices are wrong, though many people prefer one over the other. Identity-first language acknowledges that a disability is part of what makes that person who they are—it is inseparable from their identity and a connection to their community. When using identity-first language, you say "disabled person" or "autistic person." Person-first language, mentions the human before the disability; you would write a "person with a disability" or a "person with autism." In email correspondence with a disability rights activist, she assured me both options are neutral. Emily Ladau also discusses this further in her book *Demystifying Disability*. She stresses that one option is not inherently better than the other, rather it is about asking a person what they would prefer and respecting that preference. Emily Ladau, *Demystifying Disability: What to Know, What to Say, and How to be an Ally* (Berkeley, CA: Ten Speed Press, 2021), 11.
5. "Disability Impacts All of Us." Centers for Disease Control and Prevention, accessed November 29, 2023. https://www.cdc.gov/ncbddd/disabilityandhealth/infographic-disability-impacts-all.html
6. "CDC's Work on Developmental Disabilities." Centers for Disease Control and Prevention, accessed November 29, 2023. https://www.cdc.gov/ncbddd/developmentaldisabilities/about.html#:~:text=Recent%20estimates%20in%20the%20United%20States%20show,in%20physical%2C%20learning%2C%20language%2C%20or%20behavior%20areas
7. "Guidance on 'Long COVID' as a Disability Under the ADA, Section 504, and Section 1557." US Department of Health and Human Services, accessed November 29, 2023. https://www.hhs.gov/civil-rights/for-providers/civil-rights-covid19/guidance-long-covid-disability/index.html. Office for Civil Rights of the Department of Health and Human Services and the Civil Rights Division of the Department of Justice have provided guidance that long COVID is disability under Title II of the ADA, Section 504 of the Rehabilitation Act, and Section 1557 of the Patient Protection and Affordable Care Act if it substantially limits one or more major life activities.
8. "Museum Audiences Report: What Audience Finder Says about Audiences for Museums." The Audience Agency, accessed, December 11, 2023. https://www.theaudienceagency.org/asset/1995.Data. Data comes from a study of 39,318 visitors across 105 institutions in the United Kingdom.
9. "Moments That Matter: Toward a Visitor-Centered Understanding of Belonging in Museum Spaces." American Alliance of Museums, accessed November 29, 2023. https://www.aam-us.org/2023/10/26/moments-that-matter-toward-a-visitor-centered-understanding-of-belonging-in-museum-spaces/#:~:text=Moments%20That%20Matter%20to%20Belonging%20Occur%20across%20a%20Visit&text=Across%20all%20groups%2C%20moments%20of,an%20exhibit%20hall%2C%20and%20more.
10. "Assessing Attitudes of Blind Adults about Museums." MW20|Online, accessed December 1, 2023. https://mw20.museweb.net/paper/assessing-attitudes-of-blind-adults-about-museums/
11. James I. Charlton, *Nothing About Us Without Us: Disability Oppression and Empowerment* (Berkeley: University of California Press, 1998), 3.

Laureen Trainer

12. Judy Diamond, *Practical Evaluation Guide: Tools for Museums and other Informal Educational Settings* (Lanham, MD: Rowman & Littlefield, 2016), 3–4.
13. Marvin C. Alkin, *Evaluation Essentials from A to Z* (New York: The Guilford Press, 2011), 95–117.
14. This statement is based on a literature review I conducted at the start of this project. I identified fourteen books related to accessibility in museums published between 2001 and 2022 and five books focusing on museum evaluation published between 2016 and 2022. There are numerous toolkits that focus on museum accessibility available on museum websites and through organizations like the American Alliance of Museums and the Disability Rights Section of the US Department of Justice. Additionally, dozens of articles exist that highlight accessibility and evaluation in the United States and internationally. However, in my review of the literature, I did not find another book that focused specifically on evaluating accessibility in museums.
15. "Vulnerable Populations: Cognitively Impaired Research Subjects." UCI Office of Research, Human Research Protections, accessed December 4, 2023. https://research.uci.edu/human-research-protections/research-subjects/vulnerable-populations/

BIBLIOGRAPHY

Alkin, Marvin C. *Evaluation Essentials from A to Z*. New York: The Guilford Press, 2011.
American Alliance of Museums. "Museum Accessibility: An Art and a Science." Accessed November 29, 2023. https://www.aam-us.org/2022/10/21/museum-accessibility-an-art-and-a-science/
American Alliance of Museums. "The Top Ten Alliance Blog Posts of 2022." Accessed November 29, 2023. https://www.aam-us.org/2022/12/23/the-top-ten-alliance-blog-posts-of-2022/?utm_source=American+Alliance+of+Museums&utm_campaign=030b8e0384-FieldNotes_2022_Dec26&utm_medium=email&utm_term=0_-030b8e0384-%5BLIST_EMAIL_ID%5D
American Alliance of Museums. "Moments That Matter: Toward a Visitor-Centered Understanding of Belonging in Museum Spaces." Accessed November 29, 2023. https://www.aam-us.org/2023/10/26/moments-that-matter-toward-a-visitor-centered-understanding-of-belonging-in-museum-spaces/#:~:text=Moments%20That%20Matter%20to%20Belonging%20Occur%20across%20a%20Visit&text=Across%20all%20groups%2C%20moments%20of,an%20exhibit%20hall%2C%20and%20more.
American Alliance of Museums. "About Museums: Museum Facts & Data." Accessed November 29, 2023. https://www.aam-us.org/programs/about-museums/museum-facts-data/#_ednref18
The Audience Agency. "Museum Audiences Report: What Audience Finder Says about Audiences for Museums." Accessed December 11, 2023. https://www.theaudienceagency.org/asset/1995.Data
Centers for Disease Control and Prevention. "Disability Impacts All of Us." Accessed, November 29, 2023. https://www.cdc.gov/ncbddd/disabilityandhealth/infographic-disability-impacts-all.html

Centers for Disease Control and Prevention. "CDC's Work on Developmental Disabilities." Accessed, November 29, 2023. https://www.cdc.gov/ncbddd/developmental disabilities/about.html#:~:text=Recent%20estimates%20in%20the%20 United%20States%20show,in%20physical%2C%20learning%2C%20language%2C%20or%20behavior%20areas

Charlton, James I. *Nothing About Us Without Us: Disability Oppression and Empowerment*. Berkeley: University of California Press, 1998.

Diamond, Judy. *Practical Evaluation Guide: Tools for Museums and Other Informal Educational Settings*. Lanham, MD: Rowman & Littlefield, 2016.

Pressman, Heather, and Danielle Schulz. *The Art of Access: A Practical Guide for Museum Accessibility*. Lanham, MD, Rowman & Littlefield, 2021.

UCI Office of Research, Human Research Protections. "Vulnerable Populations, Cognitively Impaired Research Subjects." Accessed December 4, 2023. https://research.uci.edu/human-research-protections/research-subjects/vulnerable-populations/

US Department of Health and Human Services. "Guidance on 'Long COVID' as a Disability Under the ADA, Section 504, and Section 1557." Accessed November 29, 2023. https://www.hhs.gov/civil-rights/for-providers/civil-rights-covid19/guidance-long-covid-disability/index.html.

1

The Art of Accessible Evaluation

Heather Pressman and Danielle Schulz

Creating an accessible cultural organization (whether a museum, art center, garden, zoo, library, etc.) means enabling people with disabilities to enter and engage with its spaces, exhibitions, digital presence, and programs. Centering the needs of these audiences improves the usability and enjoyability of these experiences for everyone, both with and without disabilities.

However, creating an accessible public space is not a clear-cut process. While there are known best practices and guidelines, these are constantly evolving, can vary based on the specifics of a site, and are not always easy to locate, especially for people new to this field. For museum professionals new to accessibility work, it's typical to reach out to colleagues further along in the process for information or to seek in-depth resources they can consult, like a book. But what do you do if there is no book?

IS THERE A BOOK FOR THAT?

Several years ago, as part of our work with our local cultural access consortium, we began presenting on the topic of museum accessibility at local and regional museum conferences in and around Denver, Colorado. At the end of our presentations, one of the questions we got every time was, "Is there a book where I can learn more?" The answer, frustratingly and somewhat surprisingly, was no. Instead, we were sending session attendees away with a hodgepodge of internet links and invitations to reach out to us if they had any questions. As Toni Morrison, Beverly Clearly, and many other authors have said, if you can't find the book you want to read, then write it.[1] With this sentiment in mind, we couldn't say no to writing what became *The Art of Access: A Practical Guide for Museum Accessibility* when the opportunity arose. Finally, there would be a step-by-step introductory resource for people to turn to with their museum accessibility questions.

The Art of Access is a compilation of concrete examples and specific resources that build awareness of the disability experience, identify barriers to accessing museums, and recommend ways to dismantle these barriers and create a more accessible museum. In the book, we wanted to illuminate how accessibility can be easily integrated into the fabric of any museum, regardless of its size or budget, thus enabling their institutions to better engage with audiences. Our goals were to identify incremental ways in which museums could

Figure 1.1. *The Art of Access: A Practical Guide for Museum Accessibility* gives readers concrete steps to build an accessibility program at their museum. *Rowman & Littlefield*

Heather Pressman and Danielle Schulz

bolster accessibility—often through easy and/or low-cost activities—and share local and national resources for training, ideas, and more.

Since *The Art of Access* was published in 2021, there has been a noticeable (and long overdue) growing interest in accessibility in the field, often as an addition to existing diversity, equity, and inclusion initiatives. While many institutions began ongoing conversations about accessibility after 2016, when the American Alliance of Museums (AAM) included Diversity, Equity, Accessibility, and Inclusion (DEAI) in its strategic plan, the participants in these conversations have expanded in recent years. More museums, of increasingly varied types and sizes, are now talking about how to make their museums accessible, as are more types of museum professionals, beyond the educators who have traditionally been tasked with the work. But why the growing interest in accessibility? What does it matter if people with disabilities can engage with your offerings?

BOX 1.1. ACCESSIBILITY IN THE MUSEUM FIELD

As the leading professional organization in the museum field, many people turn to the American Alliance of Museums (AAM) for guidance and support. In February 2014, AAM signaled to its members and the field at large that diversity, equity, access, and inclusion (DEAI) were areas of importance by adopting the AAM Diversity and Inclusion Policy. In 2016, the Alliance took its commitment a step further by including diversity, equity, access, and inclusion as key areas in the strategic plan. This was followed by the publication of AAM's 2018 report entitled *Facing Change*, which "examined the characteristics of effective museum inclusion practices and considered what steps the field could take to promote DEAI."[1] DEAI continues to be one of the four areas of priority in the organization's strategic plan, which serves as a guidepost for the museum field at large.

AAM defines diversity, equity, accessibility, and inclusion as:

DIVERSITY

Diversity is all the ways that people are different and the same at the individual and group levels. Even when people appear the same, they are different. Organizational diversity requires examining and questioning the makeup of a group to ensure that multiple perspectives are represented.

EQUITY

Equity is the fair and just treatment of all members of a community. Equity requires commitment to strategic priorities, resources, respect,

(continued)

BOX 1.1. *Continued*

and civility, as well as ongoing action and assessment of progress toward achieving specified goals.

ACCESSIBILITY

Accessibility is giving equitable access to everyone along the continuum of human ability and experience. Accessibility encompasses the broader meanings of compliance and refers to how organizations make space for the characteristics that each person brings.

INCLUSION

Inclusion refers to the intentional, ongoing effort to ensure that diverse individuals fully participate in all aspects of organizational work, including decision-making processes. It also refers to the ways that diverse participants are valued as respected members of an organization and/or community.[2]

Notes

1. "Diversity, Equity, Access, and Inclusion," American Alliance of Museums, accessed September 26, 2023, https://www.aam-us.org/programs/diversity-equity-accessibility-and-inclusion/.
2. "DEIA Definitions," American Alliance of Museums, accessed January 2, 2022, https://www.aam-us.org/wp-content/uploads/2018/04/AAM-DEAI-Definitions-Infographic.pdf.

Accessibility is important first because it is the law under the Americans with Disabilities Act (ADA). Second, it is an essential part of fulfilling a museum's broader mission, ensuring that opportunities to learn are available to everyone in the community. Third, because it makes good business sense. If one in four people in the United States identifies as having a disability, consider the vast number of people who may not be coming to your museum because they cannot access its spaces, exhibitions, or programs.[2] Furthermore, people with disabilities are visiting museums with friends and family. If your museum is not welcoming and accessible, these individuals, their friends, and their families will not visit. Finally, accessibility is important because it is the right thing to do![3] Disability rights are basic human rights.[4] Visitors with disabilities have the right to inclusion, full participation, and nondiscrimination, just like any other identity group.

Heather Pressman and Danielle Schulz

BOX 1.2. UNFAMILIAR TERMS

We envision that primarily evaluators are reading this book, and therefore some of the terms used in this chapter may not be as familiar to you. These include:

Ableism—is based on the belief that nondisabled people are superior. It is defined as stereotyping, discrimination, or prejudice against people with disabilities.[1] How this shows up in a museum: inaccessible spaces and engagement formats. For example, meeting spaces are only accessible by stairs, bright lights, and/or loud noises or only providing information in a single format (e.g., only audio).

Ableist language—a linguistic microaggression, regardless of whether direct or intentional. Ableist terms exist in everyday language. Examples include "crazy," "turn a blind eye," and "dumb."[2]

Universal design—a design process aimed at creating products and environments that simplify life and are usable by as many people as possible. Universal and inclusive design is the process of embedding the choice and needs of people into the spaces and things we create. These designs are inclusive, responsive, flexible, convenient, accommodating, welcoming, realistic, and understandable. There are seven guiding principles of universal design:

- equitable use (people with diverse abilities can use the design),
- flexibility in use (can accommodate a wide range of abilities, offers choices),
- simple and intuitive use,
- perceptible information (information is effectively communicated, multiple modes of communication are used),
- tolerance for error,
- low physical effort, and,
- size and space for approach and use (components are easy to reach and use whether seated or standing).[3]

Notes

1. Rakshitha Arni Ravishankar, "Why You Need to Stop Using These Words and Phrases." *Harvard Business Review*, December 15, 2020, https://hbr.org/2020/12/why-you-need-to-stop-using-these-words-and-phrases.
2. Sara Nović, "The Harmful Ableist Language You Unknowingly Use," BBC Worklife, April 5, 2021, https://www.bbc.com/worklife/article/20210330-the-harmful-ableist-language-you-unknowingly-use.
3. "The 7 Principles," Centre for Excellence in Universal Design, accessed September 27, 2023, https://universaldesign.ie/what-is-universal-design/the-7-principles/.

WHAT IS MUSEUM ACCESSIBILITY?

While many museum professionals are familiar with the acronym DEAI and know what it stands for, not everyone understands the nuances between each of the letters. Under the ADA, accessibility means complying with the requirements of the law by removing physical barriers and providing access to communication. But other definitions, such as the one provided by AAM, broaden the meaning of access beyond physical entry to delivering relevant content and a superior user experience.[5] Overall, for museums, accessibility means providing equal access for all visitors to public programs and spaces. The goal is to eliminate most physical, communication, and policy or procedural barriers.

There are numerous ways museums can work to break down barriers to access. These can include employing universal design principles when designing spaces, exhibitions, and programs; making strides toward meaningful inclusion of the voices and perspectives of people with disabilities; confronting ableist language and practices; and sharing the responsibility across all staff for ensuring your museum is accessible. The bottom line in discussions around DEAI work is that it is important that the "A" isn't left out of the conversation.

Given how broad the field of accessibility can be, in *The Art of Access*, we tried to break it down into more manageable subcategories.[6] Specifically, we explored four overarching types of accessibility:

- Cognitive access: ensures that people with limited cognitive abilities (such as developmental or learning disabilities) can access and understand materials, communications, and other information.
- Sensory access: considers people with sensory sensitivities (including hypersensitive or hyposensitive) to environmental stimuli and how to provide both high- and low-stimuli exhibitions and experiences.
- Physical access: ensures that people with physical disabilities are able to move around and engage with the museum as intended.
- Digital access: ensures that any digital content, whether online or in the museum (such as digital interactives), is physically and cognitively accessible.

In the book, we break each of these areas down and provide examples of easy-to-scale solutions, as well as a variety of resources to help museums get started.

WHAT HAS CHANGED SINCE WE WROTE THE BOOK?

Since *The Art of Access* was published, the biggest change we've seen is a growing worldwide interest in and concern for accessibility. For example, we see more businesses than ever before that are proudly owned by or employ people with disabilities. In Denver alone, we have the Autism Community Store (the first store in the United States to specialize in products for individuals on the

Heather Pressman and Danielle Schulz

autism spectrum), Brewability (an inclusive brewery and pizzeria employing adults with disabilities to brew craft beer), and Dirt Coffee Bar (two brick-and-mortar coffee shops and programming sites that employ, train, and empower neurodivergent individuals), to name just a few.[7] Furthermore, in 2022, the Colorado Neurodiversity Chamber of Commerce was founded as the first chamber of commerce focused on creating a successful economic community for neurodiversity in business.[8]

In museums, this growing interest in inclusion is evidenced by the increased number of staff positions that have accessibility in the job description and position title, and also by a boost in the number and frequency of articles, blogs, and other media highlighting museum accessibility stories.[9] As more museums accelerate their DEAI initiatives, they are beginning to recognize that the D, E, and I are impossible without the A, and beginning to treat it as a priority—or at least part of the conversation.

One of the most noticeable changes is that accessibility concerns are now raised across many different museum departments, not just one or two. Rather than the lone voice asking questions in the past, there is now a small chorus. More museum staff are seeing how accessibility intersects with their day-to-day work, both directly and indirectly, and are taking action to make change. Exhibition designers are inviting accessibility consultations earlier and more often, visitor services teams are actively advertising access programs to visitors, and public programs staff are consistently livestreaming events with captions to accommodate home viewing, without outside requests to do so. As a result of all this growing emphasis, more museums are funneling resources into initiatives examining and adjusting current practices to improve accessibility.

ACCESSIBILITY INITIATIVES

To be successful, an accessibility initiative should follow a general four-step process:

- Step 1: Determine whether a current practice is accessible or not.
- Step 2: Make necessary changes and accommodations to practices that are inaccessible.
- Step 3: Create new policies that help institutionalize these accessible practices so that they exist beyond the present moment.
- Step 4: Evaluate the impact of these changes.

Let's use staff and volunteer training as an example of this process.

Step 1 might be to review the training schedule to see if, how often, and for whom disability awareness and etiquette training is included. It is important to note if training is only available for frontline staff or whether or not they include behind-the-scenes departments. Step 2 might be to develop and offer disability awareness training where it is lacking (either by contracting with someone to lead it or tapping into the expertise of current staff). Make this available to all staff, through recordings and open invitations. Step 3 might be to institutionalize this practice by making it an annual training, part of new employee onboarding, or some other option that standardizes this new policy into the ongoing fabric of the museum. Step 4 might be to use evaluation tools to assess the impact of the new training on staff and volunteers, gather feedback on the content and format, and even identify how it improves relationships with disabled visitors coming into the museum over the long term. This fourth step—*evaluating* accessibility initiatives—hasn't always been the norm in practice and has indeed grown in importance and relevance over the past few years, along with the increased focus on accessible practices. Yet, with a heightened focus on accessibility accommodations and more resources funneled in to create change, evaluation is important to this examination of current accessibility practices.

Following these steps will help your museum ensure that access continues to be a part of the conversations at your museum. One key thing to remember is that accessibility work is ongoing. It is a process, not a box to be checked once and forgotten. Identify incremental things you can do to promote accessibility and keep in mind that it is always better to be doing something rather than nothing!

CROSS-DEPARTMENTAL COLLABORATION

Another trend we see in museum accessibility work is increased cross-departmental collaboration to problem solve and find positive solutions for accessibility obstacles. One example of this comes from the Denver Art Museum (DAM). Over the past several years, DAM staff noticed an increase in visitation from adult day centers, particularly on the museum's monthly free days. Staff embraced this as a positive development illustrating that the museum was increasingly seen as a welcoming and engaging place for people with disabilities to visit. However, as a result of this uptick, a challenge arose. These groups, usually consisting of ten to twenty visitors, often arrived with prepacked lunches but had no designated area in which to eat them. They began to sit at the on-site café, which is relatively small given the overall size of the museum, and only has a few seats available, which needed to be reserved for people buying lunch. This resulted in some small conflicts and discomfort; more than once, museum staff had to ask the groups to leave the café if they were not purchasing any food.

So, what to do? Representatives from DAM's operations department invited its accessibility coordinator to a small working meeting, where together they identified the problem (clogged seating in the café) and discussed a solution that would meet the needs of these groups: increasing the number of tables and seating on free days. They then instituted a new policy to have these additional tables and chairs set out each free day, which resulted in a greater

Heather Pressman and Danielle Schulz

sense of welcome and inclusion for these day groups. And, as is so often the case with accessible practices, this extra seating also benefits other visitors, such as families with small children, older adults, and college groups.

STAFF ACCESSIBILITY

We've also seen a growing consideration of museum staff's own accessibility needs. For so many years, museums have put all their energy into meeting visitors' needs, sometimes to the detriment of staff. (Anyone who has worked a free day can attest to this!) Recently, however, there has been growing awareness of the needs and rights of staff, including disabled staff. Human resources and accessibility teams are increasingly working together to care for the accessibility needs of the organization's staff.

As with any accessibility initiative, supporting the needs of staff with disabilities starts with asking questions about current practices. For example:

- Are staff offices held to the same physical accessibility standards as the public museum spaces, with accessible doors and ramps to enter?
- Is your employee-orientation information available in multiple modalities (for example, on paper, digitally, and orally)?
- Have you considered providing sensory tools (like weighted neck pillows, noise-reducing headphones, and fidget toys) to support neurodiverse museum staff during their working hours, the same way you might provide them to visitors inside the museum? (This could have an especially positive impact on staff on the front lines during high-volume days.)

In addition to supporting their existing staff's accessibility needs, museums are also taking steps to make their hiring practices more inclusive to those with disabilities. This can include practices like detailing on job postings what to expect in the hiring process (for example, the number of interviews expected and the format they will take place), and even sharing interview questions beforehand to support applicants who may need more time to prepare.

Focusing on accessibility within the museum can help change attitudes about employing people with disabilities at museums and at the very least foster dialogue around these important issues. As many museums are working to address staff burnout by focusing on wellness and retention, inclusive practices like these can help make a healthier culture and working environment for everyone.

WHAT MAKES EVALUATION ACCESSIBLE?

Until recently, it was uncommon for accessibility initiatives to include an evaluation step. As the work has grown, however, museum practitioners have come to see it as a crucial part of the process, to ensure any changes are having the intended impact. Likewise, as evaluation has grown as a museum practice, evaluators have come to see the need to incorporate accessibility lenses in their work.

Dialogue is an essential component of both accessibility and evaluation, and this book is unique in bringing the two fields into dialogue to reveal how they can benefit one another. The chapters included here highlight how evaluation and accessibility can work together toward the shared goal of engaging visitors in quality experiences.

There are two main ways to think about the intersection between these fields: implementing accessible evaluation practices and evaluating accessibility programs and accommodations. We'll now tease apart these two areas to see the opportunities and pitfalls of each.

QUESTION, REFLECT, MODIFY: ACCESSIBLE EVALUATION PRACTICES

According to the American Evaluation Association, evaluation is a "systematic process to determine merit, worth, value, or significance."[10] Inside museums, the evaluation process generally looks like asking questions, reflecting on information, and making modifications based on that information. When collecting information from visitors, museums are asking questions and listening to feedback. The information being collected can range in topic and scope depending on the root of the issue, from big picture questions (Who is coming to our museum? What are they interested in?) to more specific inquiries (What do visitors think about the history of brewing exhibition? Has the pinwheel-making program achieved what it set out to?). An accessible line of evaluation questions might expand the scope of the question (Who is coming to our museum and what are the accessibility accommodations that can be most beneficial?) and consider a wider audience demographic (What do visitors, both with and without disabilities, think about the science of soufflé exhibition?).

Accessible practices can start from the beginning of the evaluation process by training data collectors on disability-inclusive language, etiquette, and methods of positively interacting with visitors with disabilities. This way, they will know how to shape evaluation tools like surveys, interviews, observations, and focus groups to be inclusive from the outset. For example, they might choose to provide surveys in multiple languages (including Braille and American Sign Language) and in different modalities (for example, on paper, digitally, and orally). When conducting interviews and observations, if evaluators are trained on disability etiquette, they may better understand how different behaviors may look during the observation. For example, a visitor on the autism spectrum may not make direct eye contact with an interviewer. This is not distracted behavior or a sign of disrespect. Rather, it may be stressful or uncomfortable for the individual to make prolonged eye contact, and avoiding this can actually help them focus

Heather Pressman and Danielle Schulz

on the task at hand. It is equally important to be intentional with focus group representation and recruitment. Are disability voices (literally) being heard and included as part of the stakeholder group? Are closed captions, CART and ASL interpreters present to support the D/deaf and hard of hearing community to follow and contribute to the conversation? For visitors who may be nonverbal, is space made for them to utilize communication devices? Including diverse voices and opinions can support evaluators to better align with community needs and interests.

Museums utilize evaluation when making decisions and determining priorities. If evaluation practices remain inaccessible to visitors with disabilities and these rich perspectives remain overlooked, museums will continue to be inaccessible and unwelcoming spaces not prioritized by people with disabilities. Diverse perspectives can also inform the modifications and decisions that museums make based on this collected feedback. Evaluative thinking helps to set goals and determine specific outcomes, and evaluation measures if and when these have been achieved. Yet, if evaluation mindset and tools are inaccessible to people with disabilities and not inclusive of their viewpoints and experiences, how can the information they collect truly be considered comprehensive or even accurate? Take, for example, the big-picture evaluation question, "Who is coming to our museum?" This is meant to determine demographics (age, gender, location, etc.). The information collected is used to make decisions around priorities (where to allocate budget, hire staff, apply for grants). If a museum notices that a large number of visitors are families with young children, they may decide to focus their resources on developing early childhood content and programs. A museum may do this by including a survey question asking respondents if they are visiting with any young children (0-5) today and offer a yes/no answer. Or, they could be more specific: Are you visiting with any young children today? Check all that apply: birth to 1 year old, 2–3 years old, 4–5 years old. So too it would follow that this same museum might increase the number of programs and content for people with vision impairments (audio guides, verbal descriptions tours) if they learned instead that a large number of visitors were blind or had low vision. However, they would need to collect data on this community, like they did with families. This might mean something as general as adding a survey question that asks if someone in the group identifies as having a disability. Or, if the museum wanted to know about a range of disabilities, they could ask the following: Would accommodations in any of the following areas have benefitted someone in your group today? Check all that apply. A list may include: physical/mobility, visual, hearing, developmental, intellectual, autism spectrum disorder, and dementia/memory loss. Or, if the museum was specifically focused on visitors with low vision, an initial question might ask if the visitor, or someone in their group, has low vision, a visual impairment, or is blind. A follow-up question could then ask about accommodations. Which accommodations would be helpful to you/your group in the galleries? Check all that apply: audio guides, verbal tour descriptions, large print, screen readers, Braille labels, touch objects, as starting examples.

A word of warning here: As you begin this journey, the general museum survey may show very few people who identify as disabled. However, this makes sense in context—your museum may not have welcomed disabled people and their families previously, your galleries and programs may not have been accessible, or your museum may not have started building bridges with disabled communities. So, it makes sense that the percentage of visitors who identify as disabled is currently low. Do not use this as a reason not to embark on an accessibility journey, but rather a baseline as you begin to welcome more people with disabilities.

WHAT IS SUCCESS? EVALUATING ACCESSIBILITY INITIATIVES

Evaluation helps museum staff answer the question, "What is success?" by providing evidence about what is working and what is not working within a certain exhibition, program, or other element. For example, if we were to say that this is the most accessible book ever written and is making a positive impact on readers, how would we know this to be true? Without evidence to point to and build our case, there would be no way to prove the validity of these statements. Accordingly, if museums want to understand their impact on disability communities, they must build evaluation capacity to collect feedback about their practices.

Evaluative thinking can help institutions drive meaningful outcomes from accessibility initiatives. This starts with identifying intended outcomes at the beginning of a project, so it is possible to define and measure success at the end. For instance, in the above example where a museum wanted to create an in-gallery program for low-vision and blind visitors, staff might identify that outcome as visitors deepening their appreciation of how artists use texture to imbue their art with emotion or gaining a better understanding of how paleontologists clean and cast dinosaur bones in the field. With these outcomes in mind, staff could work with members of the blind and low-vision community to brainstorm ways to accomplish these outcomes. For the texture project, they may decide that high-contrast wall text, verbal description tours, and touch objects will help them achieve the intended outcome. For the paleontology project, they may decide to offer audio guides describing each step of the process, install a screen reader on any touch screens documenting fieldwork, and turn up the lights in the section of the gallery featuring a recreated dig site to make that area brighter.

Evaluation then helps to determine if the museum was successful (or not, or only partially) in achieving its outcomes, and what role the various accommodations played (or didn't play) in leading to success. For example, measuring metrics like usage statistics, satisfaction ratings, and visitor observations can help staff understand how and to what extent visitors are using accommodations during their museum visits, and then use the findings to spur program improvement. But be careful! You must consider all your evaluation findings in context. For example, low-usage numbers may simply indicate a lack of awareness, not a lack of interest. Before concluding that tools or programs are unsuccessful, you might consider how you can increase awareness, such as including more in-gallery information about their availability, making them more prominent and inviting, training staff and/or guards to talk about them, or developing a marketing campaign about them.

This is also when employing interviews and focus groups is crucial. Usage statistics, satisfaction ratings, and observations are great tools and often are a great starting point, but they have their limitations. They don't allow you to dig deeper and ask follow-up questions: Why did you do this? Why didn't you use that? How could the design/language/video/audio/interactive be improved in a way that is beneficial to you? What were you thinking when you read/saw/interacted with that? What else would have helped you? These are the types of questions that require that you talk to the visitors to try and understand their actions, their thoughts, and what adjustments to the space and offerings may provide an even better experience that leads to richer outcomes. From our example above, the survey results leave you with a question: Does the low uptake of sensory tools in the gallery point to low interest or low awareness? Interviews and focus groups can provide crucial context to survey data to help ensure that the data is interpreted correctly. And importantly, participants can play a role in brainstorming iterations and solutions.

Evaluation data can also help inform good decision making under the constraints of typical museum operations. Faced with tight budgets and limited staff capacity, museums are constantly determining where to focus resources to make the biggest impact. The data and stories collected during evaluation projects can help make the case for (or against) dedicating budget and staff time to continuing accessibility initiatives or identify strategies for continuing them while managing capacity. For example, an uptick in sensory tool usage during summer months may prompt a museum to allocate more staff resources and funds to maintaining the tools during this time of year compared to others.

When embarking on an evaluation project for an accessibility program, knowing how to interpret the data, and who to partner with to help interpret it, is just as crucial to collecting the feedback. We've mentioned the importance of meaningful inclusion of disability voices and perspectives, and this is paramount when collecting and interpreting feedback on accessibility initiatives. Embracing the adage "nothing about us without us" means asking your community what success means to them.[11] This is not to minimize your expertise as an evaluator but to embrace the opportunity to share authority and create the biggest impact. From the beginning, consult with disability community members for whom your program is intended on what the program outcomes should be and how to measure them. Success for many accessibility initiatives isn't purely a numbers game. For example, some programs may max out at twenty participants due to space constraints. So how can you accurately measure value? If you can, employ a professional from the disability community to consult, help you collect information, review the interview questions, or even recruit participants. This could be a great opportunity to partner with workforce development programs to give disabled youth job-readiness experience.

As you'll read within the case studies in this book, programs that increase access to museum spaces for people with disabilities have far-reaching impacts on these communities. Evaluation is the way to uncover, understand, and articulate those impacts. By meeting disabled visitors where they are, museums are becoming more welcoming and increasing feelings of belonging. At the same time, they are having positive impacts on visitors without disabilities who can also benefit from these programs and accommodations. Finally, they are supporting staff by helping them do their jobs better, increasing the awareness and understanding of disability experiences and needs, and the museum's role in supporting them. And how do we know this? Through evaluation. The data and stories collected during evaluation projects can help illuminate the impact of a museum's work. Evaluation truly is a form of storytelling through statistics, data, and words.

EVALUATING ACCESSIBILITY, ACCESSIBLY EVALUATING

Just as *The Art of Access* was born out of need, this book was born out of a need to explore the intersection between accessibility and evaluation. As museum professionals, we use evaluation to make decisions about whether we are going to continue a program, what an event might look like next year, what sorts of exhibitions our community might want to attend, and more. Taking the time to make sure that your evaluation practices are inclusive of people with disabilities and that your accessibility programs are evaluated ensures that your work is comprehensive and inclusive and continues to champion accessibility. The case studies included within this book give insight into accessible evaluation efforts that we hope will inspire your own practice.

NOTES

1. Jeffrey Davies, "Writing What You Need to Read: One Quote Shared by Countless Authors," BOOK RIOT, April 21, 2022, https://bookriot.com/who-said-writing-what-you-need-to-read/.
2. "Disability & Health Data System," Center for Disease Control and Prevention, accessed January 3, 2022, https://www.cdc.gov/ncbddd/disabilityandhealth/dhds/index.html; for more information on invisible disabilities, please see Chapter 6 of *The Art of Access: A Practical Guide for Museum Accessibility* by Heather Pressman and Danielle Schulz.

3. Betty Siegel, Keynote Address, Art of Access Symposium, Denver, July 12, 2017. Betty Siegel is the director of VSA and accessibility, and she is the force behind the global LEAD® conference (Leadership Exchange in Arts and Disability) from the John F. Kennedy Center for the Performing Arts.
4. "Promoting the Rights of Persons with Disabilities," accessed September 10, 2023, https://www.state.gov/promoting-the-rights-of-persons-with-disabilities/.
5. "DEAI Definitions,"American Alliance of Museums, accessed January 2, 2022, https://www.aam-us.org/wp-content/uploads/2018/04/AAM-DEAI-Definitions-Infographic.pdf.
6. In any conversation about accessibility, it is important to understand the history behind accessibility as a civil right. Before engaging in this work, we recommend starting out by learning about the history of the disability rights movement. This topic is covered briefly in chapter 1 of *The Art of Access: A Practical Guide for Museum Accessibility* by Heather Pressman and Danielle Schulz. Kim Nielsen's *A Disability History of the United States* is also an excellent source.
7. For more on these organizations, please visit their websites: https://autism communitystore.com/, https://brew-ability.com/, https://www.dirtcoffee.org /about-us 9/12/23
8. "Home," Colorado Neurodiversity Chamber of Commerce, accessed September 1, 2023, https://www.cndcc.org/.
9. The germination for this book came from the blog post "Museum Accessibility: An Art and a Science" written for AAM's *Alliance Blog* by many of the contributors to this book. https://www.aam-us.org/2022/12/23/the-top-ten-alliance-blog -posts-of-2022/
10. "What Is Evaluation?," American Evaluation Association, accessed September 26, 2023, https://www.eval.org/About/What-is-Evaluation.
11. James I. Charlton, Nothing About Us Without Us: Disability Oppression and Empowerment (Berkeley: University of California Press, 1998.) JSTOR, www.jstor .org/stable/10.1525/j.ctt1pnqn9.

BIBLIOGRAPHY

American Alliance of Museums. "DEAI Definitions" Accessed January 2, 2022. https://www.aam-us.org/wp-content/uploads/2018/04/AAM-DEAI-Defi nitions-Infographic.pdf.
American Evaluation Association. "What Is Evaluation?" Accessed September 26, 2023. https://www.eval.org/About/What-is-Evaluation.
Center for Disease Control and Prevention. "Disability & Health Data System." Accessed January 3, 2022. https://www.cdc.gov/ncbddd/disabilityandhealth/dhds/ index.html.
Centre for Excellence in Universal Design. "The 7 Principles." Accessed September 27, 2023. https://universaldesign.ie/what-is-universal-design/the-7-principles/.
Colorado Neurodiversity Chamber of Commerce. "Home." Accessed September 26, 2023. https://www.cndcc.org/.
Davies, Jeffrey. "Writing What You Need to Read: One Quote Shared by Countless Authors." BOOK RIOT, April 21, 2022. https://bookriot.com/who-said-writing-what -you-need-to-read/.

Nović, Sara. "The Harmful Ableist Language You Unknowingly Use." BBC Worklife, April 5, 2021. https://www.bbc.com/worklife/article/20210330-the-harmful-ableist-language-you-unknowingly-use.

Pressman, Heather and Danielle Schulz. *The Art of Access: A Practical Guide for Museum Accessibility.* Lanham, MD: Rowman & Littlefield, 2021.

Ravishankar, Rakshitha Arni. "Why You Need to Stop Using These Words and Phrases." *Harvard Business Review*, December 15, 2020. https://hbr.org/2020/12/why-you-need-to-stop-using-these-words-and-phrases.

Siegel, Betty. Keynote Address. Art of Access Symposium. Denver, July 12, 2017.

US Department of State. "Promoting the Rights of Persons with Disabilities–United States Department of State." January 19, 2021. https://www.state.gov/promoting-the-rights-of-persons-with-disabilities/.

2

Centering First-Person Perspectives in an Exhibit Accessibility Audit

Sarah Brenkert, Malikai Bass, Dillyn Adamo, and Ellie Kravets

In 2021, the Seattle Aquarium partnered with graduate students at the University of Washington to complete an accessibility audit and examine engagement within an interpretive exhibit at the aquarium. Though the aquarium's internal evaluator originally conceived the study as a standard front-end evaluation gathering background data on visitation patterns, the university team reimagined the scope to center questions of accessibility and inclusion as critical measures of exhibit effectiveness. The team—which included people who identify as having a disability, as disability advocates, or both—developed an evaluation plan that prioritized the voices and perspectives of disabled people and used a mixed-methods approach that included timing and tracking observations, reflective interviews, and a priority audience focus group. Findings resulted in near- and long-term recommendations for increasing accessibility through physical modifications, signage and graphics updates, and integration of accessibility technologies.

This chapter will describe this collaborative effort between the aquarium and the University of Washington (UW) evaluation team, which resulted in a study that analyzed barriers to accessibility and brought first-person voices from the community into access conversations— challenging the aquarium to seek more authentic approaches to inclusion in the process.

THE AQUARIUM SEEKS TO BROADEN ITS REACH

Built on Piers 59 and 60 of Seattle's central waterfront (Dzidzilalich), the Seattle Aquarium stands literally knee-deep in the Salish Sea, one of the world's largest and most biologically diverse inland seas. The name of the Salish Sea honors the Coast Salish people, original inhabitants of the region who have stewarded its land and waters since time immemorial—and continue to do so today.

With a relatively small physical footprint, Seattle Aquarium is nonetheless among the busiest aquariums in the United States, with more than twenty-seven million visitors since its opening in 1977. Formerly owned and operated by the City of Seattle Department of Parks and Recreation, the aquarium has been managed by the nonprofit Seattle Aquarium Society since 2010, which now operates it as a 501(c)(3). Accredited by the Association of Zoos and Aquariums, the Seattle Aquarium comprises six major galleries focused on marine ecosystems of the Pacific and sees more than eight hundred thousand visitors each year. The aquarium employs approximately 280 full- and part-time staff members, including a full-time conservation engagement and learning evaluator (a position held by coauthor Sarah Brenkert during this project).

Over the last ten years, the social context in which zoos and aquariums exist has changed profoundly, transformed by heightened awareness of the climate crisis, the sweeping effects of the COVID-19 pandemic, a rise in advocacy for racial justice, and a growing awareness of how environmental conservation and social justice intersect. In April 2023, the White House issued an executive order (E.O 14096: *Revitalizing Our Nation's Commitment to Environmental Justice for All*) acknowledging what black, Latino, Indigenous, and other grassroots community advocates have long argued: that many communities with a significant portion of low-income residents, disabled individuals, and people of color "experience disproportionate and adverse human health or environmental burdens . . . [and] face entrenched disparities that are often the legacy of discrimination and segregation, redlining, exclusionary zoning, and other discriminatory land use decisions or patterns."[1]

Challenged by community partners and staff members to demonstrate a commitment not just to environmental conservation but to justice, the Seattle Aquarium has taken public positions on antiracism and environmental justice, and prioritized community-focused relationality. In 2018, the aquarium developed a new set of organizational values, including one dedicated to becoming a more inclusive community:

> We view diversity as a strength and recognize that we can only achieve our mission by including the skills and varied perspectives of all people. We understand that environmental burdens and benefits are not equitably distributed and that we have a responsibility to foster inclusive conversations about our marine environment. We strive to create a more welcoming and equitable culture as we work together to fulfill the Aquarium's mission.[2]

The aquarium is currently working under a twenty-year strategic plan, which includes the goal of significantly increasing both the physical size of the aquarium's campus and its accessibility to the community. As the aquarium organization actively works toward the opening its expanded campus—including the massive new Ocean Pavilion building—there is an elevated awareness of the need to prioritize accessibility in both existing and new spaces. Accessibility objectives within the organization's strategic plan include the following:

- Creating a system of communication for guest experiences focusing on inclusion and accessibility.
- Creating an inclusive website experience with easily accessible information for audiences seeking accommodations.
- Embodying our "Inclusive Community" value by developing and implementing training in antiableist and antiracist communication for all staff.
- Developing an audience demographic data collection plan to systematically assess who is and isn't served by the aquarium.
- Defining and implementing strategies to intentionally invite, welcome, and support audiences we have historically marginalized and excluded in the past.
- Partnering with communities to support experiences that honor their priorities and interests.
- Optimizing the aquarium's built environment and facilities for universal access.[3]

The last three objectives relate specifically to the evaluation efforts described in this chapter. The aquarium recognizes that both tangible and intangible barriers to accessibility continue to exist and impact our community. By initiating an accessibility audit and collecting data about the nature of these barriers, the organization sought to make progress toward the strategic and ethical imperative of universal access. The difficult truth that continued to elude us, however, was that our mindset toward evaluation—its structure, its mechanisms, and its purpose—remained steeped in dominant culture and ableist assumptions.

PARTNERSHIP WITH THE UNIVERSITY OF WASHINGTON

In 2021, the University of Washington's Master of Arts in Museology program publicly circulated a call for proposals inviting local cultural organizations to submit outlines for collaborative evaluation studies. The call noted that the selection process would prioritize evaluation studies exploring issues of diversity, equity, inclusion, and access. Around the same time, members of the aquarium's internal exhibits committee (including the vice president of facilities and operations, visitor engagement interpreters, graphic designers, vice president of life sciences, animal care staff, and the internal evaluator) were discussing

BOX 2.1. UNIVERSITY OF WASHINGTON MASTER OF ARTS IN MUSEOLOGY PROGRAM

The University of Washington's museology graduate program is a two-year, full-time program based on the university's main Seattle campus. The program defines its focus broadly to encompass nonformal learning centers of all kinds—including zoos, aquariums, natural history museums, science centers and parks—stating, "museums are part of a much larger informal learning infrastructure, a community ecology that includes libraries, community-based organizations and more. We focus on transferrable skills across this ecology" (About–Museology Master of Arts Program [washington.edu]).

The University of Washington is the only museum studies graduate program in North America offering a specialization in museum evaluation. Students pursuing the specialization focus on evaluation theory, data collection, interpretation and analysis techniques and principles, and collaborative inquiry to help address critical questions that arise within museums and informal learning contexts. Program director, Jessica Luke, emphasizes that a large part of the evaluation specialization's purpose is to train professionals with skills to "interrogate the practices and processes that shape museums, and to elevate the voices of audiences and community within organizations" (Jessica Luke, personal communication).

Students in the evaluation specialization spend their second year in the program developing and implementing a year-long evaluation study in collaboration with a partner cultural organization. Partner organizations are selected each year through a request for proposal (RFP) process in which interested museums submit a draft project outline framing the intended focus of the evaluation and describing its relevance and utility for the organization.

the need to critically assess areas of the existing building that were older or considered "underperforming" and determine the scale of renovation necessary to bring them in line with more recently developed spaces.

The aquarium's internal evaluator, Sarah Brenkert, was at maximum capacity with other projects and unable to take on any new studies of that scope. Reflecting on the need for data to inform redesign efforts, and the institutional desire to prioritize access in its facilities planning, the aquarium decided to submit a proposal to the museology program for a front-end exhibit evaluation of the *Sound to Mountain* exhibit space. Brenkert coordinated meetings of the aquarium team and served as point of contact for the museology students.

Figure 2.1. Molalla, a North American river otter, rests on a rocky ledge in his habitat inside the Seattle Aquarium. *Seattle Aquarium*

BOX 2.2. SOUND CHOICES GRAPHIC PANEL

Along with a flowing freshwater stream display, a small viewing pane looking over Elliott Bay, and the Aquarium's North American river otter habitat, Seattle Aquarium's Sound to Mountain exhibit also houses a 70-foot long infographic panel known as *Sound Choices*, a graphic installation co-developed with the National Oceanic and Atmospheric Administration (NOAA) in 2014 and intended to help the public explore how individual and collective choices shape the future of our waterways.

In 2016, the *Sound Choices* installation in the Sound to Mountain gallery was the subject of another Museology evaluation study that examined engagement with the panels and take-aways related to conservation actions. The study collected only a small amount of data about the exhibit overall, but found that Aquarium visitors tend to move quickly through the area and suggested that accessibility barriers may affect visitor choices and experience.

Figure 2.2. A view of the river otter habitat from across the Sound to Mountain corridor. The walkway is approximately 9′ wide at its widest point and 5′ wide at its narrowest.
Seattle Aquarium

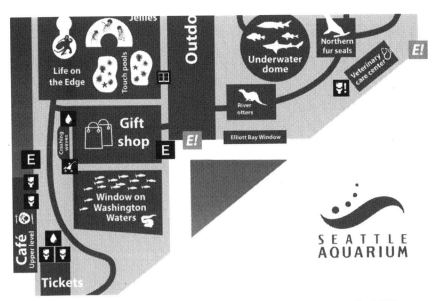

Figure 2.3. The Sound to Mountain area is highlighted in this section of a 2023 Seattle Aquarium visitor map. Directly across from the river otter habitat is a small viewing window to Elliott Bay. The freshwater stream display and the Sound Choices graphic installation are not labeled on this map, but are located near the restroom and the Veterinary Care Center. *Seattle Aquarium*

Sound to Mountain is a narrow gallery that serves as a primary circulation corridor as well as home to a freshwater stream display and the aquarium's North American river otter habitat. The aquarium staff identified a set of evaluation priorities for the space focused on the visitor experience, with the "typical" visitor tacitly assumed to be a person without visible or invisible disability. The aquarium's initial evaluation questions were these:

- What are the patterns of movement and flow in the space?
- How long do people typically stay in this space?
- What elements and features draw visitors' attention?
- How do people engage with these elements? (e.g., stop, read, point, touch)
- What, if anything, do people find memorable or meaningful about the space?

While these evaluation questions aren't inherently wrong or bad, in retrospect, we can now see they reflect a subtle ableist mindset, focusing on "visitors" as an undifferentiated aggregate. Time-strapped program staff and busy evaluators will likely recognize the forces at play here; a decision *not* to enumerate specific audiences is often based on limitations of time and resources, or on difficulty in recruiting representative samples. The decision to use a convenient sample of "most" as a proxy for "all" visitors is a common practice in informal learning settings and might seem like a relatively inconsequential—if obtuse—omission. However, failing to make specific inquiries into the experience of people with disabilities reveals a set of assumptions that are far more pernicious: that minority or marginalized groups do not have experiences that differ from majority experiences in any important ways, and/or that methods designed to measure experiences of dominant culture audiences (in this case nondisabled visitors) will magically measure experiences of marginalized groups too. The mental schema that underpins those original evaluation questions is the same that perpetuates the construct of *normalcy*—where nonconforming human traits and abilities are relegated to the margins, deemed less consequential than conforming ones, or even a deviation or defect from them. As Lennard J. Davis writes in *Enforcing Normalcy: Disability, Deafness, and the Body*, "The problem is not the person with disabilities; the problem is the way that normalcy is constructed to create the problem of the disabled person."[4]

Despite the shortcomings of the original proposal, museology graduate students Malikai Bass, Dillyn Adamo, and Ellie Kravets saw potential for the study, and elected to partner with the aquarium to design and execute an accessibility evaluation of the *Sound to Mountain* space. The first step in developing an evaluation plan for the exhibit was to find common ground for all stakeholders on what issues and questions would be centered in the study. Bass, Adamo, and Kravets set an agenda for the project's kick-off meeting in October 2021 that prioritized two tasks: co-creating a statement of purpose for the project and articulating the evaluation questions that would guide the study's design and methodology.

To begin the meeting, the museology team thoughtfully but candidly shared their concerns about the assumptions implicit in the original proposal. They urged aquarium staff to examine our assumptions about who our "typical visitors" are, sharing data from the Centers for Disease Control and Prevention (CDC) that "approximately one in four adults (25.7%) in the United States, or 61 million people, reports living with at least one disability. Women, older adults (≥ 65 years), American Indians/Alaska Natives, [and] adults with lower income . . . are more likely to have a disability."[5]

When aquarium staff suggested adding an evaluation question to explore possible barriers to access in the exhibit, the student team embraced the idea and encouraged the group to be precise and specific in thinking about issues of access, avoiding the pitfall of referring to all types of physical, social, and intellectual disabilities in aggregate. Kravets recalls, "That was one of the big concerns we had: different facets of accessibility all getting lumped together under the heading of accessibility. Because when you start talking about accessibility that broadly, it's very easy to get into places of conflicting accommodation needs, and by talking about everything you're really talking about nothing. It's hard to effectively examine different facets of accessibility within a single study."[6]

Throughout the initial meeting, Bass, Adamo, and Kravets continued to demonstrate the breadth of their knowledge of disability justice, and aquarium staff recognized that as disability advocates (Adamo and Kravets) and a person with a disability (Bass), their experience and expertise should drive the study and set the direction for its design. Out of that meeting, the student team developed an evaluation purpose statement and four guiding questions that integrated the aquarium's priority interests about exhibit effectiveness with a specific focus on access and the experience of visitors with disabilities (see box 2.3).

UNIVERSITY PARTNERS BRING LIVED EXPERIENCE AND DISABILITY RIGHTS PERSPECTIVE TO STUDY

Bass, Adamo, and Kravets felt encouraged by the openness and flexibility demonstrated by the aquarium. The three students noted they had recently worked on another accessibility-related project with a different partner but found it frustrating due to organizational resistance that limited the amount of change they could effect. They expressed relief that the aquarium was receptive to their suggestions about refining the study's aims and appeared to respect their knowledge and lived experience. Describing that initial meeting to kick off the project, Kravets recalled thinking that the aquarium staff showed that they were "willing to work with us to find a model of disability and a model of

**BOX 2.3. SOUND TO MOUNTAIN EVALUATION
PURPOSE STATEMENT AND EVALUATION QUESTIONS**

Evaluation Purpose Statement

The purpose of this study is to gain an understanding of general visitor experience and the specific experiences of disabled visitors in the Sound to Mountain exhibit space. This study will be used to make long- and short-term recommendations for this space.

Evaluation Questions

1. What environmental and content barriers do visitors experience in the Sound to Mountain exhibit space?
2. Specifically, how and to what extent do these barriers impact the experiences of disabled visitors within the exhibit?
3. How do different visitors engage with exhibit components?
4. What major themes/messages are visitors taking from their Sound to Mountain exhibit experience?

inclusion and accessibility that was going to work for all of us."[7] She added, "Transparently, we would have fought you on that if you weren't willing to see the need for that."

Bass agreed, stating, "Accessibility has always been a huge focus of my museum and general academic practice as a disabled person. It was a reoccurring theme throughout my work in the museology program, so I was really excited to have something that would be situated within that for the evaluation project."[8]

As the collaboration progressed, the student team supported aquarium staff's growth and learning around disability justice and the sociopolitical theory that underpins the movement. When explaining her team's approach to the study design, for instance, Kravets offered this summary:

> There are a few classic models of disability. What still tends to be used in a lot of spaces is a medical model of disability which defines disability as a failing of an individual's body to do something that is considered typical. It places the fault with the person, rather than as a societal obligation to fix the problem. There are other models of disability that fall into a social model of disability where society is responsible for creating spaces and processes that accommodate a variety [of] abilities and ways of moving through the world. In this social model, disability is seen as just another facet of identity and not an inherent failing or deficit.[9]

The medical model of disability that Kravets references (sometimes known as the "individual model" of disability, because of its emphasis on the individual as the "problem") maintains that disabilities are physical or cognitive deficits that require medical care or "correction" by expert interventions. Another model the team rejected is the "charity model," which portrays people with disabilities as vulnerable and reliant on people without disabilities, effectively denying them agency and humanity. At the same time, as disability activist A. J. Withers has written, the charity model often leans into the narrative of disabled persons as engaged in a noble struggle, "brilliantly co-opting the language of resistance by talking about 'fighting,' 'resisting,' and 'beating' disabilities."[10]

The model Kravets holds in contrast, the "social model" of disability, has roots in the disability rights movement emerging from the 1960s and 1970s, including the work by the Union of the Physically Impaired Against Segregation (UPIAS), one of the first political advocacy groups set up and controlled by disabled people.[11] Mike Oliver, a British sociologist, author, and disability rights activist, coined the term "social model of disability" in 1981 and helped shift the paradigm from one of individual "defects" to environmental and attitudinal conditions that erect barriers and marginalize people. The social model of disability construes disability "as a socially constructed phenomenon" rather than an individual failing or personal tragedy.[12]

While this model was instrumental in bringing about landmark policy changes like the United Nations' 1993 Standard Rules on the Equalization of Opportunities for People with Disabilities[13] and the United States' 1990 Americans with Disabilities Act, many disability activists and disabled self-advocates argue that we still need additional tools and heuristics to advance the emancipatory goals of the disability community.[14] Therefore, new models have arisen to extend beyond the advances of the social model. As Bass explained to us, "In a lot of my work I use a rights-based model of disability and an identity/cultural (socio-political model) of disability. These models are foundational for disability justice perspectives and disability criticism. These models involve thinking about access to museums/aquariums as places that should be equally accessible to all social groups including disabled people as a default."[15]

The "identity model" Bass points to is closely related to the social model of disability but emphasizes affirmation, claiming disability a positive identity.[16] Brewer and colleagues distinguish the identity model from the social model in these terms:

Under the identity model, disability is a marker of membership in a minority identity, much like gender or race . . . [W]hile the identity model owes much to the social model, it is less interested in the ways environments, policies, and institutions disable people, and more interested in forging a positive definition of disability identity based on experiences and circumstances that have created a recognizable minority group called "people with disabilities."[17]

Sarah Brenkert, Malikai Bass, Dillyn Adamo, and Ellie Kravets

The "rights-based model" of disability also emphasizes the cultural and community membership aspects of disability and advocates for equitable access across social and political contexts.

While thinking through these models of disability may seem like an unnecessary theoretical exercise, our experience has taught us that it's a crucial first step in any accessibility initiative. Whether we have named them or not, each of us—and our organizations collectively—hold and operate under a model of disability, and proceeding without examining what it is can do more harm than good. Retief and Letšosa describe multiple ways our implicit and explicit paradigms shape practice, including the following:

- Providing definitions of disability
- Providing explanations of causal attribution and responsibility attributions
- Defining (perceived) needs
- Guiding the formulation and implementation of policy
- Determining which academic disciplines study and learn about people with disabilities
- Shaping the self-identity of people with disabilities
- Causing prejudice and discrimination[18]

ADVANCING AN INCLUSIVE RESEARCH PARADIGM

As the collaboration moved forward, the student team came to trust that the aquarium was willing to hear critical feedback, and aquarium staff continued to show up with humility, open to examining and revising our assumptions. In December 2021, the student team presented a new evaluation plan to center the voices of people with disabilities, which introduced the idea of the "inclusive research paradigm," a model first described by Walmsley and Johnson in 2003.[19] Bass, Adamo, and Kravets explained that this paradigm was developed in collaboration with self-advocates with disabilities, and seeks to return power to disabled people and respect their agency by ensuring they are full participants in designing research that benefits them—rather than simply serving as subjects.[20, 21] This means disabled individuals are involved in every step of the research, including conceiving of questions and collecting data, with the goal for the research to actively serve the priorities of these participants in terms of both process and outcomes. The students sought to bring the voices of disabled people to bear in multiple phases of the work, including the following:

- study design, instrument development, data collection, analysis, and interpretation
- input and insight regarding the lived experiences of disabled individuals (from study participants recruited from the Seattle-area disability community)

As Adamo put it, "We wanted to do something meaningful. Especially in evaluation work, there can be ways in which data can be used to perpetuate harm or create a deficit framework for communities. So we were eager to have the opportunity to center the disabled community first and foremost and work on a project that might actually have a positive influence on the museum world."[22]

METHODS AND FINDINGS

The team proposed a mixed-methods approach to collecting data. They identified two subgroups of study participants: general visitors who have chosen to come to the aquarium and a purposive sample of nonvisitors from within the Seattle-area disability community. They planned to collect data for these two groups in phases, with Phase 1 focusing on reflective interviews and timing and tracking with general visitors and Phase 2 consisting of a focus group comprising participants recruited through the students' personal and organizational networks, including Disability Rights Washington and the Student Disability Commission at the University of Washington. The team initially scheduled the Phase 2 focus group to take place in person but encountered significant reluctance among participants to travel to the aquarium and gather in an enclosed space because of COVID concerns. Ultimately, the team revised the plans and held a virtual focus group with disabled-identifying individuals.

METHOD ONE: TIMING AND TRACKING (N=81)

To support the aquarium's interest in learning how visitors navigate, use elements, and spend time in the *Sound to Mountain* area, the evaluation team agreed to use a systematic observation protocol known as timing and tracking. Timing and tracking is a method often used in free-choice learning spaces to understand how visitors navigate a space and how long they spend in different areas.[23] For timing and tracking studies, researchers count and document visitors' patterns of behavior and engagement as they explore exhibit or galleries, and use other indicators (such as gestures, facial expressions, photography, and social interactions) to make inferences about visitor interest and engagement.

While they acknowledge the utility of this method in their study, Bass, Adamo, and Kravets emphasized that timing and tracking is acutely limited as a way of understanding the visitor experience—especially that of disabled visitors. First, they argued, because timing and tracking records are not designed to identify visitors with and without disabilities. The data is based on the observations and perceptions of the data collector(s), rather than self-reported information from the visitors, who may not immediately or obviously present as disabled. As N. Ann Davis emphasizes in her 2005 paper, "Invisible Disability," "There are many individuals with conditions, illnesses, and structural or biomechanical anomalies that are life limiting but not readily discernible to others."[24] For that reason, external observation cannot offer full insight into how visitors with and without disabilities experience a space differently. Additionally, timing and tracking records have the potential for misinterpretation. For example, while visitors spending longer in certain areas could be due to heightened enjoyment and engagement, it could also indicate a barrier or difficulty that needs to be addressed. Finally, timing and tracking studies often focus on physical navigation and may overlook other types of barriers, such as cultural, sensory, or cognitive barriers.

Having established the limitations of this method, the evaluation team planned to collect timing and tracking data onsite through in-person observation in *Sound to Mountain*. However, after touring the space with aquarium staff, Bass, Adamo, and Kravets realized that the layout, size, and ambient conditions posed significant barriers to accessibility for team members. Specifically, because *Sound to Mountain* functions as both an exhibit space and a circulation pathway, it is a narrow and often congested area. It also lacks seating or places for rest and has a high level of noise from visitor movement, conversations, and the flowing water of the freshwater stream display.

As a solution to these barriers, the aquarium decided to give the students access to view its closed-circuit camera footage, an approach that the organization had never used in evaluation studies before. By viewing both live and recorded camera footage, Bass, Adamo, and Kravets observed visitors as they passed through the *Sound to Mountain* exhibit space and documented dwell time and engagement behaviors on a standard visit tracking form (see figure 2.4).

We did not need any intentional recruiting methods for this method since the population of interest was already visiting the exhibit. To notify visitors of the study, we placed a stanchion-mounted sign at both entrances to the exhibit stating that observation was occurring via cameras and directing visitors who wished to opt out toward a different exit. For each observational record, data collectors recorded contextual information about the visit, such as exhibit crowding, group composition, and the presence or absence of mobility aids such as wheelchairs, walkers, canes, strollers, and/or service animals.

Their records revealed that 73 percent of timing and tracking subjects were part of a group with at least one child (defined as someone who appeared to be younger than eighteen), and 15 percent were part of a group with someone who used or carried a mobility aid. On average, the visitors they observed spent two minutes and thirty-three seconds in the *Sound to Mountain* space and spent the most time at the river otter habitat (average: a little over one minute).

The freshwater stream display had the next highest dwell time, with an average of twenty-eight seconds. The other elements of the exhibit space—the "Sound Choices" graphic panel and the Elliott Bay Window opening to the water below the aquarium—had much shorter engagement times. When accounting for participants that spent no time engaging with these exhibit components, the median dwell time was near zero seconds, indicating that these elements were frequently skipped. (See Figure 2.6 for median engagement time at all exhibit elements.)

APPENDIX C

Timing & Tracking: Instrument

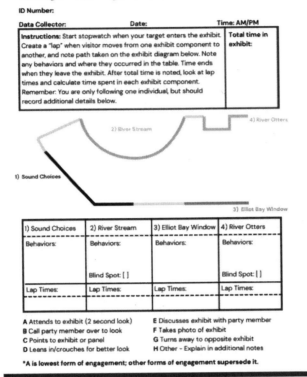

ID Number:

Data Collector: Date: Time: AM/PM

Instructions: Start stopwatch when your target enters the exhibit. Create a "lap" when visitor moves from one exhibit component to another, and note path taken on the exhibit diagram below. Note any behaviors and where they occurred in the table. Time ends when they leave the exhibit. After total time is noted, look at lap times and calculate time spent in each exhibit component. Remember: You are only following one individual, but should record additional details below.

Total time in exhibit:

2) River Stream

4) River Otters

1) Sound Choices

3) Elliot Bay Window

1) Sound Choices	2) River Stream	3) Elliot Bay Window	4) River Otters
Behaviors:	Behaviors:	Behaviors:	Behaviors:
	Blind Spot: [ ]		Blind Spot: [ ]
Lap Times:	Lap Times:	Lap Times:	Lap Times:

A Attends to exhibit (2 second look)   E Discusses exhibit with party member
B Call party member over to look   F Takes photo of exhibit
C Points to exhibit or panel   G Turns away to opposite exhibit
D Leans in/crouches for better look   H Other - Explain in additional notes

*A is lowest form of engagement; other forms of engagement supersede it.

Figure 2.4. Page 1 of Bass, Adamo, and Kravets' timing and tracking data collection form. Questions about group size and composition, estimated visitor age and use of mobility devices was recorded on a second page. *Adamo, Bass and Kravets (2022)*

Timing & Tracking: Time Spent in Exhibit

Participants spent an average of **2 minutes and 33 seconds** in the Sound to Mountain exhibit space.

Participant spent the **longest average time engaging** with the **river otters,** spending around a minute with this exhibit component.

Figure 2.5. High level findings about visitor dwell-time from Sound to Mountain timing and tracking study. *Adamo, Bass and Kravets (2022)*

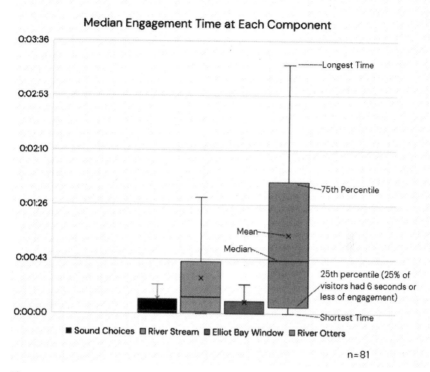

Figure 2.6. Median engagement time at each off the elements in the Sound to Mountain gallery. *Adamo, Bass and Kravets (2022)*

METHOD TWO: REFLECTIVE INTERVIEW (N=50)

Reflective interviewing is a qualitative data collection technique that involves talking with participants after an experience and using artifacts, images, or other visual/sensory tools to prompt recollection and analysis.[25] For the reflective interviews in *Sound to Mountain*, Bass, Adamo, and Kravets positioned themselves near the exit of the exhibit space. Their shifts varied by day (weekday/weekend) and time (morning/afternoon) to account for the widest possible swath of generalized visitor experience in the exhibit. As groups exited, they invited them to participate and walked those who agreed through a series of interview questions, including some that addressed issues of accessibility, using an exhibit map as needed to prompt or provide context.

Following the reflective tracking questions, they also asked about perceived themes and content takeaways from the exhibit. Finally, they gave an optional demographics survey to each visitor participating in the interview, with ques-

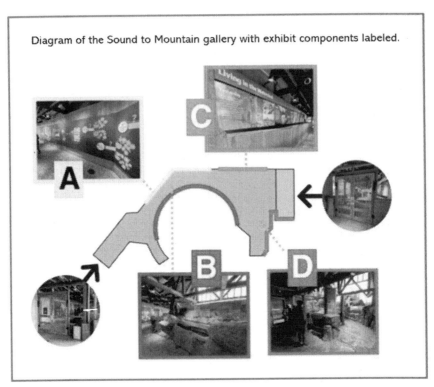

Diagram of the Sound to Mountain gallery with exhibit components labeled.

Figure 2.7. This diagram of the Sound to Mountain gallery was printed on 24" x 36" foamcore and mounted on an easel near the intercept location for reflective interviews. Participants could refer to the different zones and exhibit components in their conversations with data collectors. *Adamo, Bass and Kravets (2022)*

tions addressing group composition, ages, disability status, language(s) spoken at home, and typical visit frequency.

Most participants in the reflective interviews were visiting for the first time (78 percent), and most self-identified as between the ages of eighteen and thirty-five (63 percent). Ninety-two percent did not identify as disabled, while 6 percent self-identified as d/Deaf, b/Blind, disabled, or having a disability. (Two percent preferred not to disclose that information.)

The majority of participants did not report experiencing barriers to physical, environmental, or conceptual accessibility in the *Sound to Mountain* exhibit space. (See figure 2.8.) However, the evaluation team posits that the results for these questions likely reflect substantial positivity bias (i.e., participants felt reluctant or otherwise uncomfortable to disclose access barriers they experienced in the exhibit.) For similar investigations in the future, we may consider transitioning from a Yes/No/Explain question, as it was styled in this study, to a self-reported, scaled question.

The majority of participants **did not** report experiencing barriers to **physical, environmental,** or **conceptual** accessibility in the *Sound to Mountain* exhibit space.

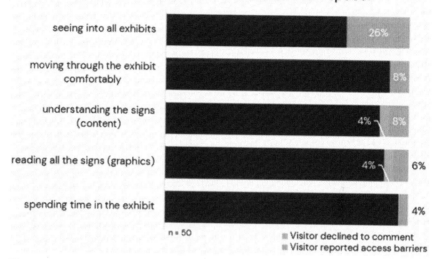

seeing into all exhibits — 26%

moving through the exhibit comfortably — 8%

understanding the signs (content) — 4% / 8%

reading all the signs (graphics) — 4% / 6%

spending time in the exhibit — 4%

n = 50

■ Visitor declined to comment
■ Visitor reported access barriers

Figure 2.8. Stacked bar chart showing the proportions of visitors who did and did not report experiencing barriers to engagement in Sound to Mountain.
Adamo, Bass and Kravets (2022)

With that as a caveat, it's useful to note that 26 percent of respondents indicated they could not see into some part of the exhibit. When probed, the barrier they most frequently reported was that the walls were too tall to allow them to effectively see in. Other visibility issues they cited included that lighting wasn't adequate to see animals, acrylic panels were clouded with spray or water marks, and that the exhibit was too crowded to see certain elements. Additionally, 10 percent of respondents stated they could not move comfortably or freely in the space, and 8 percent indicated the exhibit area provoked sensory discomfort.

METHOD THREE: VIRTUAL FOCUS GROUP (N=2)

Initially, the evaluation plan called for a series of in-person focus groups with four to six members of the disability community each, but recruiting participants proved challenging. The focus groups were slated to take place between January and March of 2022, a time when the United States was experiencing the initial omicron wave of COVID-19, which "involved the highest weekly number of cases and nearly the highest weekly number of deaths of the entire pandemic," according to analysis from Johns Hopkins University.[26] This period was especially concerning for people with disabilities, who often have a higher risk of infection from the disease "because of underlying medical conditions, or systemic health and social inequities," as the CDC notes.[27] When recruiting potential participants, Bass, Adamo, and Kravets received feedback that pandemic-related concerns, specifically around utilizing public transit and gathering in communal spaces, were a significant deterrent to participation. In response to these concerns, they made the decision to use a virtual format instead.

BOX 2.4. PLANNING FOCUS GROUPS THAT ARE WELCOMING, ACCESSIBLE, AND INCLUSIVE FOR PARTICIPANTS WITH DISABILITIES

Making focus groups accessible to people with disabilities is crucial for ensuring inclusivity and gathering diverse and representative perspectives. Here are some things to consider when planning for more accessible experiences.

Planning and Preparation

- **Accessible venue**: Choose a location that is wheelchair accessible, with accessible restrooms and parking. Ensure the space is navigable for people with mobility aids.
- **Assistive technologies**: Provide assistive listening devices, screen readers, or other technologies as needed.
- **Skilled facilitation**: The facilitator should be trained in inclusivity and sensitive to the needs of all participants.

Communication Accommodations

- **Sign language interpreters**: For participants who are deaf or hard of hearing, provide sign language interpreters.
- **Microphones and amplification**: Establishing a norm of speaking only when using a microphone minimizes cross-talk and side conversations. Using a microphone also provides support for assistive listening devices (such as a hearing loop).
- **Captioning**: Offer real-time captioning for spoken content.
- **Clear and simple language**: Use clear, concise language and avoid jargon. Provide materials in easy-to-read formats.
- **Varied communication options**: Allow participants to express themselves in different ways, such as speaking, writing, or using communication boards.

Visual and Auditory Accommodations

- **Large print and Braille materials**: Offer all printed materials in large print and Braille versions.
- **Visual aids**: Use high-contrast visuals and avoid overloading slides with information.
- **Appropriate lighting**: Ensure the room has adequate lighting, especially for those with visual impairments.

Flexible Formats

- **Consider virtual**: If a conversation can be held online, it may eliminate barriers to participation such as resource restrictions and the ability or willingness of participants to travel.
- **Accessibility tools**: If the focus group is online, ensure the platform is accessible, with options for keyboard navigation, screen reader compatibility, and captioning.
- **Breakout sessions**: For in-person meetings, consider smaller breakout groups to balance the sensory stimulation of larger settings.
- **Flexible timing**: Be flexible with the timing, allowing participants to take breaks as needed. This is important for all participants, especially those with fatigue-related disabilities.

Feedback and Improvement

- **Postsession feedback**: After the focus group, seek feedback specifically about the accessibility of the session to learn and improve for future sessions.

In the end, this revised approach resulted in a single online focus group with just two participants from the disability community. This was a smaller sample than the evaluation team had hoped to attain, so we emphasized from the beginning that the resulting data would be primarily exploratory and descriptive, rather than conclusive. Both participants in the focus group reported that they visited the aquarium a few times a year, independently or with friends and family. Both had successfully completed a bachelor's degree, were between the ages of eighteen and thirty-five, and spoke English as their primary language. Both were compensated for their time with tickets to the Seattle Aquarium and a ten-dollar Tango card.

During the focus group, the participants viewed photos and videos depicting the *Sound to Mountain* gallery as well as a Zoom live stream Adamo hosted from their smartphone to guide participants through elements of

Preparation

1	Use evaluative methods and existing community connections to highlight potential barriers to discuss and to develop questions that comprehensively cover exhibit accessibility. Consider questions about physical access, sensory environment, path finding, label context, visual contrast, and physical supports.
2	Use a high quality camera to take photos of all exhibit elements, signage, and pathways in normal conditions. Human models allow visitors to better understand scale and placement. Ensure photos and videos are representative of an average visit rather than the "best experience".
3	Connect with community partners to recruit and schedule meetings using zoom. Be sure your zoom room has key accessibility features such as closed captioning and chat enabled. After picking a date, hire captioners or interpreters as needed.
4	Prepare an agenda, script and slideshow which incorporates the developed questions and the photo and video content [See Appendix]. Prepare a digital survey to gather needed demographic information or information required to deliver compensation.
5	Conduct a pilot test to capture potential technology or accessibility issues. Ensure the live video streaming is clear, comprehensible, and responsive to questions/directions from the zoom meeting.

Figure 2.9. Planning notes and suggestions developed by Bass, Adamo, and Kravets for developing more inclusive focus group. *Adamo, Bass and Kravets (2022)*

interest. The facilitators asked questions about their experiences in similar spaces and invited them to reflect on accessibility barriers they might anticipate within the space.

Based on what they saw, participants identified several aspects of the exhibit as potential barriers based on their access needs. For example, Participant A shared that "the exhibit expects you to walk through it the entire time without saying, 'Oh hey, maybe you need a break.'" They found this lack of rest opportunities especially daunting knowing that the exhibit was on the far side of the institution from the entrance, "where you're more likely to be fatigued." Participant B highlighted a lack of visibility and ease of seeing/using signs and labels: "Some of the font does seem a little small because there's big chunks . . . If I were in a chair or something, I wouldn't be able to see and read the top parts."

The participants also provided recommendations based on their experiences visiting museums and similar settings. Participant A shared, "I tend to

Sarah Brenkert, Malikai Bass, Dillyn Adamo, and Ellie Kravets

get fatigued really easily, so having benches, or something similar, in easily accessible spots makes it so I know I'm not going to have to leave early if I need to rest." Participant B recommended "very clear signage [pointing to where] there are certain areas to sit," particularly for larger venues.

STUDY CONCLUSIONS

While the study yielded valuable data on how barriers within the exhibit impact the experiences of disabled visitors, the evaluators acknowledge that their efforts were hampered by the significant underrepresentation of disabled individuals in the reflective interview population (6 percent versus a population average of 27 percent[28]) and the small sample size of the virtual focus group (n=2). In some ways, this limited sample was an important finding in itself, as it suggests additional barriers may persist, limiting or discouraging disabled individuals from visiting the *Sound to Mountain* exhibit or the Seattle Aquarium as a whole.

Despite these limitations, Bass, Adamo, and Kravets documented a number of findings related to accessibility concerns in *Sound to Mountain*, including the following:

- length of labels
- lack of seating
- height and color of signs and other exhibit components
- noise created by the stream and waterfall
- narrow and uneven pathways
- potential for crowding

These barriers, which impact the experience of all visitors, have a more pronounced impact on disabled visitors by compounding existing fatigue and stress.[29,30] They may mean disabled visitors are less likely to linger in the exhibit space or interact with all components, potentially impacting both their enjoyment and learning outcomes within the space.

The team also captured a number of recommendations from the study, some of which could be implemented in the short term and others that would require a longer time horizon or more comprehensive renovation. Some of the short-term recommendations included updating the doors to the exhibit space, which currently lack accessible handles and automatic door openers; integrating additional seating options; and adding signs to help visitors anticipate the high levels of ambient noise and irregular floor texture in the space. Longer-term recommendations included refreshing or replacing signage with high-contrast colors and dyslexia-friendly fonts and reorganizing the space so there is no longer interpretive content and/or animal habitats on both sides of the corridor, which creates complications for traffic flow and accessibility.

THE IMPORTANCE OF FIRST-PERSON PERSPECTIVE IN EVALUATION

Designing and implementing an evaluation centered on an inclusive research paradigm was possible because of the knowledge, experience, and commitment of the students leading the project. The aquarium's key contributions were in recognizing the importance of bringing in first-person perspectives from members of the disabled community and sharing power and authority in the design of the study. The underrepresentation of disabled individuals in the study sample and the challenges in recruiting focus group participants from the disabled community suggest there may be complex and abiding factors that continue to pose barriers to full accessibility. However, this study demonstrates that there are simple steps—starting with evaluation planning and continuing through data collection—that can be taken within any project to prioritize the participation and perspectives of the disability community.

NOTES

1. Joe Biden, "Executive Order 14096: Revitalizing Our Nation's Commitment to Environmental Justice for All," The White House, 2023. https://www.whitehouse.gov/briefing-room/presidential-actions/2023/04/21/executive-order-on-revitalizing-our-nations-commitment-to-environmental-justice-for-all/.
2. "Our S.A.L.I.S.H Values: what we stand for," Seattle Aquarium. 2018, https://www.seattleaquarium.org/what-we-stand-for.
3. "Strategic Plan 2011–2030," Seattle Aquarium. 2010, [internal document].
4. Lennard J. Davis, *Enforcing Normalcy: Disability, Deafness, and the Body* (London: Verso, 1995; rpt. 2000), 23–24.
5. Catherine A. Okoro, NaTasha Hollis, Alyssa Cyrus, Shannon Griffin-Blake, "Prevalence of Disabilities and Health Care Access by Disability Status and Type Among Adults—United States, 2016," *Morbidity and Mortality Weekly Report* 67, no. 32 (2018): 882–87.
6. Ellie Kravets, personal communication.
7. Dillyn Adamo, personal communication.
8. Malikai Bass, personal communication.
9. Ellie Kravets, personal communication.
10. A. J. Withers, "The Charity Model/Revolution," 2012, Accessed September 7, 2023, https://stillmyrevolution.org/2012/01/01/the-charity-model/revolution.
11. Colin Barnes and Geof Mercer, "Chapter 1." In *Implementing the Social Model of Disability: Theory and Research* ed. Colin Barnes and Geof Mercer (Leeds: The Disability Press, 2004), 1–17.
12. Marno Retief and Rantoa Letšosa, "Models of Disability: A Brief Overview." in *HTS Teologiese Studies/Theological Studies* 74, no. 1 (2018): a4738.
13. "Standard Rules on the Equalization of Opportunities for Persons with Disabilities." United Nations Office of the High Commissioner, last modified 1993. Accessed September 1, 2023. https://www.ohchr.org/en/instruments-mechanisms/instruments/standard-rules-equalization-opportunities-persons-disabilities.
14. Mike Oliver, "Changing the Social Relations of Research Production?" *Disability, Handicap & Society* 7, no. 2: (1992): 101.

15. Malikai Bass, personal communication.
16. Elizabeth Brewer, Brenda Jo Brueggemann, Nicholas Hetrick, and Melanie Yergeau, "Introduction, Background, and History," in *Arts and Humanities*, ed. B. Brueggemann (Thousand Oaks, CA: Sage Press, 2012), 27.
17. Brewer et al., 5.
18. Retief and Letšosa, "Models of Disability," a4738.
19. K. Johnson and J. Walmsley, *Inclusive Research with People with Learning Disabilities: Past, Present and Futures* (London: Jessica Kingsley Publishers, 2003), 45.
20. Eleanor Lisney, Jo Bowen, Ken Hearn, and Maria Zedda, "Museums and Technology: Being Inclusive Helps Accessibility for All" *Curator: The Museum Journal*, 56, no. 3 (July 2013): 353–61.
21. Marilina Mastrogiuseppe, Leandro Guedes, Stefania Span, Patrizia Clemente and Monica Angela Landoni, "Reconceptualizing Inclusion in Museum Spaces: A Multidisciplinary Framework," conference presentation at the 14th annual International Conference of Education, Research and Innovation, November 2021. Accessed September 1, 2023, https://library.iated.org/publications/ICERI2021.
22. Dillyn Adamo, personal communication.
23. Steven S. Yalowitz and Kerry Bronnenkant, "Timing and Tracking: Unlocking Visitor Behavior," *Visitor Studies* 12, no. 1 (Spring 2009): 47–64. https://doi.org/10.1080/10645570902769134.
24. Davis, *Enforcing Normalcy*, 24.
25. Renee Spencer, Julia Price, and Jill Walsh, "Philosophical Approaches to Qualitative Research," in *The Oxford Handbook of Qualitative Research,* ed. P. Leavy (Oxford University Press, 2014), 86.
26. "COVID-19 in 2022: A Year-End Wrap-Up," Johns Hopkins University, accessed October 2, 2023, https://publichealth.jhu.edu/2022/covid-year-in-review#:~:text=In%202022%2C%20COVID%2D19%20illness,a%20major%20wave%20of%20cases.
27. "People with Disabilities: Vaccine Information," Centers for Disease Control and Prevention, accessed September 30, 2023, https://www.cdc.gov/ncbddd/humandevelopment/covid-19/people-with-disabilities.html.
28. "Disability Affects Us All," Centers for Disease Control and Prevention infographic, accessed August 8, 2023, https://www.cdc.gov/ncbddd/disabilityandhealth/infographic-disability-impacts-all.html.
29. Elizabeth Guffey, "The Disabling Art Museum." *Journal of Visual Culture,* 14, no. 1 (April 2015): 61–73.
30. Caroline Van Doren, Peter-Willem Vermeersch, and Ann Heylighen. "Understanding Museum Architecture from Disability Experience" in *Contemporary Museum Architecture and Design: Theory and Practice of Place,* ed. Georgia Lindsey (New York: Routledge, 2020), 167–68.

BIBLIOGRAPHY

Barnes, Colin and Geof Mercer. "Chapter 1." In *Implementing the Social Model of Disability: Theory and Research,* edited by Colin Barnes and Geof Mercer, 1–17. Leeds: The Disability Press, 2004.

Biden, Joe. 2023. "Executive Order 14096: Revitalizing Our Nation's Commitment to Environmental Justice for All." The White House. https://www.whitehouse .gov/briefing-room/presidential-actions/2023/04/21/executive-order-on-revitaliz ing-our-nations-commitment-to-environmental-justice-for-all/.

Brewer, Elizabeth, Brenda Jo Brueggemann, Nicholas Hetrick, and Melanie Yergeau. "Introduction, Background, and History." In *Arts and Humanities,* edited by Brenda Jo Brueggemann, 1-62. Thousand Oaks, CA: Sage Press, 2012.

Centers for Disease Control and Prevention. "Disability Affects Us All." Accessed August 8, 2023. https://www.cdc.gov/ncbddd/disabilityandhealth/infographic-disabil ity-impacts-all.html.

Centers for Disease Control and Prevention. "Disability and Health Data System." Accessed August 8, 2023. http://dhds.cdc.gov.

Centers for Disease Control and Prevention, "People with Disabilities: Vaccine Information." Accessed September 30, 2023. https://www.cdc.gov/ncbddd/humandevelop ment/covid-19/people-with-disabilities.html.

Davis, Lennard J. *Enforcing Normalcy: Disability, Deafness, and the Body.* London: Verso, 1995. Reprint, 2000.

Guffey, Elizabeth. "The Disabling Art Museum." *Journal of Visual Culture* 14, no. 1 (April 2015): 61-73.

Johns Hopkins University. 2022. "COVID-19 in 2022: A Year-End Wrap-Up." Accessed October 2, 2023. https://publichealth.jhu.edu/2022/covid-year-in-review#:~:text =In%202022%2C%20COVID%2D19%20illness,a%20major%20wave%20of%20 cases.

Johnson, K., and J. Walmsley. *Inclusive Research with People with Learning Disabilities: Past, Present and Futures.* 1st ed. London: Jessica Kingsley Publishers, 2003.

Lisney, Eleanor, Jo Bowen, Ken Hearn, and Maria Zedda. "Museums and Technology: Being Inclusive Helps Accessibility for All." *Curator: The Museum Journal.* 56, no. 3 (July 2013): 353-61.

Mastrogiuseppe, M., L. Guedes Soares, S. Span, P. Clementi, and M. Landoni. "Reconceptualizing Inclusion in Museum Spaces: A Multidisciplinary Framework." In ICERI2021 Proceedings (2021), 7225-233. https://library.iated.org/publications/ICERI2021.

Mastrogiuseppe, M., S. Span, and E. Bortolotti. "Improving Accessibility to Cultural Heritage for People with Intellectual Disabilities: A Tool for Observing the Obstacles and Facilitators for the Access to Knowledge." *Alter* 15, no. 2 (April 2021): 113-23.

Okoro, C. A., NaTasha Hollis, Alyssa Cyrus, Shannon Griffin-Blake. "Prevalence of Disabilities and Health Care Access by Disability Status and Type Among Adults—United States, 2016." In *Morbidity and Mortality Weekly Report* 67, no. 32 (2018): 882-87.

Oliver, M. "A New Model of the Social Work Role in Relation to Disability." In *The Handicapped Person: A New Perspective for Social Workers?* edited by J. Campling. London: RADAR (1981): 20-37.

Oliver, M. "Changing the Social Relations of Research Production?" *Disability, Handicap & Society* 7, no. 2 (1992): 101-14.

Retief, M., and R. Letšosa. "Models of Disability: A Brief Overview." *HTS Teologiese Studies/Theological Studies* 74, no. 1 (2018): a4738.

Spencer, R., J. M. Pryce, and J. Walsh. "Philosophical Approaches to Qualitative Research." In *The Oxford Handbook of Qualitative Research,* edited by P. Leavy, 81-98. Oxford University Press, 2014.

United Nations Human Rights Office of the High Commissioner. December 1993. "Standard Rules on the Equalization of Opportunities for Persons with Disabilities." Accessed September 1, 2023. https://www.ohchr.org/en/instruments-mechanisms /instruments/standard-rules-equalization-opportunities-persons-disabilities.

Van Doren, Caroline, Peter-Willem Vermeersch, and Ann Heylighen. "Understanding Museum Architecture from Disability Experience." In *Contemporary Museum Architecture and Design: Theory and Practice of Place*, ed. Georgia Lindsey (New York: Routledge, 2020), 167–68.

Withers, A. J. 2012. "The Charity Model/Revolution." Accessed September 7, 2023. https://stillmyrevolution.org/2012/01/01/the-charity-model/revolution.

Yalowitz, Steven S., and Kerry Bronnenkant. "Timing and Tracking: Unlocking Visitor Behavior." *Visitor Studies* 12, no. 1 (April 2009): 47–64. https://doi.org/10 .1080/10645570902769134.

Zhao, Guixiang, et al. "Prevalence of Disability and Disability Types by Urban–Rural County Classification—U.S., 2016." *American Journal of Preventive Medicine* 57, no. 6 (2019): 749–56.

3

Access from the Ground Up

DESIGNING A MUSEUM FACILITY WITH ACCESS IN MIND

Lisa Eriksen, Tina Keegan, and Maia Werner-Avidon

> "The new JMZ blew my mind. I have never before seen such thoughtful consideration of every member of our community. Every detail said, 'I see you.'" —Junior Museum & Zoo Visitor (family with a child with a disability)[1]

> "I loved the very big, obvious inclusion of all. Keep making it BIG! People have needs and not all needs are the same." —Junior Museum and Zoo Visitor (family with a child with a disability)[2]

In 2021, the Palo Alto Junior Museum & Zoo (JMZ) opened a new facility designed to offer a truly accessible and inclusive experience that goes far beyond what is required by the Americans with Disabilities Act (ADA). The new facility—with building design by CAW Architects, zoo design by SH|R Studios, and in-house exhibit design—was the culmination of more than thirteen years of accessibility work by the institution. Working closely with an accessibility advisory team composed of parents of children with disabilities, adults with disabilities, and disability advocates—and incorporating staff training and exhibit prototyping throughout the design process—the JMZ has created a new facility that meets the needs of all members of the community, with positive impacts even for families where no one has a disability.

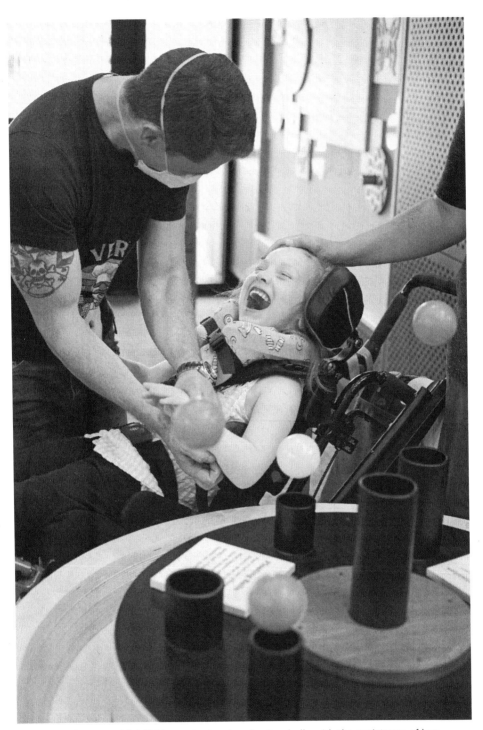

Figure 3.1. A young girl delights as she touches floating balls with the assistance of her parents. This child has multiple disabilities, and the various accommodations at the JMZ support her access to the experiences. Her parents suggested the addition of adult-size changing tables in the restrooms. *Eron Truran*

THE NEED FOR ACCESS

People with disabilities are the country's largest minority group, and a significant number of these people are children with physical and cognitive disabilities. Recent data from the US Centers for Disease Control and Prevention estimates that about one in six children ages three through seventeen have one or more developmental disabilities or delays, a number which is increasing over time.[3] About one in thirty-six children has been diagnosed with autism spectrum disorder.[4] The state of California follows these national trends, with more than eight hundred thousand K–12 students enrolled in special education in 2022-2023.[5] Currently, the most common disabilities students enroll for are learning disabilities and speech or language impairments, but autism is one of the most significant areas of growth.[6]

Despite this prevalence, most museums do not go beyond the minimum legal standards required by the ADA in their approach to disability. The 2010 report *Inclusion, Disabilities and Informal Science Learning* by the Center for the Advancement of Informal Science Education (CAISE), for instance, found that "projects, initiatives, and organizations that have sought greater inclusion of people with disabilities in [informal science education] . . . are still the exception and not the rule."[7] The report concluded that informal science education needed to go:

> further than ensuring that people with disabilities can enter the buildings or use the exhibits, programs, and technologies that deliver such experiences . . . [to ensuring they can] learn from such experiences and participate as a part of, and not separate from, the larger social group and community.[8]

It is this vision of inclusion that has guided the JMZ on its accessibility journey.

THE JMZ'S ACCESSIBILITY JOURNEY

Founded in 1934, the JMZ is the oldest children's museum west of the Mississippi, with a small zoo later added in 1969. It is a small, community-based institution owned and operated by the City of Palo Alto (California) and supported by a volunteer nonprofit fundraising organization. Its mission is to engage a child's curiosity in science and nature through hands-on activities and interaction with live animals. Most visitors are families with children between the ages of zero to nine, with the majority being children ages five or under.

Since the JMZ is operated by a small staff (nine full-time and thirty-five part-time), there is no formal evaluation department. Historically, the museum has conducted evaluation as part of specific projects or initiatives and used it to inform direction and decisions. Staff in the education and exhibition departments usually lead the work, or an outside evaluator for some grant-funded projects. For exhibitions, the museum generally conducts front-end, formative, and summative evaluations. Prototyping and testing exhibits are core parts of the exhibit development process.

As proof that failure really can lead to innovation, the JMZ's accessibility and inclusion journey began with a failed grant application in 2010. The application proposed a number of initiatives to better serve children with disabilities, including an accessible exhibition and a focus group. While management staff supported inclusion, there was no staff member dedicated to accessibility at the time, and most accessibility efforts—including this grant application—were championed by the exhibits director. While the application ultimately did not result in funding, staff decided to move forward regardless with a focus-group-style "Community Conversation." Led by an external evaluator, Wendy Meluch of visitor studies services, the conversation included people who were parents of, or who served, children with disabilities. Participants shared their gratitude at being involved. In the words of one parent:

> I think I can say for all of us, how much we appreciate you even asking. Just the fact . . . that you bothered to ask means that this is available to me again. We just have so many places that don't care or don't bother. Maybe it's just benign neglect, but the fact that you asked is really important to us as a community. It's huge!

From this early conversation emerged the idea of offering a special event for families who have children with disabilities—which would require only that the facility either open a little earlier or close later than normal. Deciding the idea was worth a try, core staff baked some muffins, invited some board members, and spread the word to the families and organizations they had met with. It was an incredible turnout! Families were grateful, staff and board members saw the impact firsthand, and the kids had a wonderful time in a quieter setting with the exhibits and animals. This initial event became the beginning of a popular series the museum now calls Super Family Sundays, which the museum has continued to offer regularly for the past thirteen years.

In the meantime, staff began to put other feedback and information collected at the Community Conversation to work, researching accessibility best practices, engaging volunteers with disabilities, and adding an accessibility page to the museum's website. Then, in 2011, when the organization embarked on a master planning and capital campaign to replace its aging eighty-plus-year-old facility, staff recognized a prime opportunity to make the facility more inclusive and accessible. Since the museum was completely rebuilding and redesigning everything, they could design for access from the ground up. In 2015, a $25,000 grant from the David and Lucile Packard Foundation helped the JMZ ramp up these efforts by providing five staff accessibility trainings and engaging universal design and ADA consultants in master planning for the new museum building and zoo. The two consultants, ACT Services and Kanics Inclusive Design Services, recommended following universal design principles, developing an ADA checklist and policies, improving signage (through elements like font size, illustrations, and Braille), and taking a multisensory exhibits approach.

Later that year, the museum held two more Community Conversations onsite at the JMZ—one for parents of children with autism and another for parents of children with physical and cognitive disabilities. To find parents to participate, staff reached out to JMZ members and visitors and local organizations, offering fifty-dollar gift cards as an incentive. Ten to thirteen parents participated in each conversation. While they met with the evaluator Meluch, staff provided hands-on, educational programming and snacks to the children and their caregivers. The ninety-minute conversations were semistructured, guided by specific questions developed by Meluch and the JMZ staff, but the format was conversational, offering opportunities to ask follow-up questions in order to delve deeper into hot topics. These conversations confirmed the findings of the 2010 Community Conversation but dug deeper, listening to a wider range of concerns and needs from this diverse audience.

Participants described their challenges with access in local museums and shared their specific needs. Their recommendations included physical and social access to exhibits, improved access for children who are blind or visually impaired, a quiet place for visitors with autism, additional staff training, and continued engagement in the design process. Meluch captured the conversations in a summary report that she shared with staff, who have used it to support ongoing inclusion work and grant applications.

After years of prioritizing inclusion, the JMZ leadership understood it was critical to embed the value deeper into the museum's institutional culture as it prepared for rebuilding and reopening. This began with developing a comprehensive inclusion plan with input from the disability community, which was fully integrated into the JMZ's strategic plan in 2016. The plan outlines goals, core principles of accessibility, and strategies in areas like human resources, policies, guest services, exhibits and zoo experiences, and programs. It articulates the vision statement that:

> The new JMZ will be a truly inclusive museum and zoo where children with disabilities and their caregivers feel welcome. Experiences will engage the inner scientist in all children by utilizing universal design to support physical and developmental needs and learning styles. Not only will all children be able to access the JMZ—children of all abilities will feel delight and inspiration while sharing the experience with their classmates, friends and family.

In 2017, the Institute of Museum and Library Services awarded $270,000 to fund the Access from the Ground Up (AGU) project, through which the JMZ worked to address the lack of quality science learning experiences for children with disabilities and their families through the development of an accessibility advisory team, ongoing staff training, and the development of new permanent exhibits, respite spaces, and other access resources for the new museum and zoo.

ACCESS FROM THE GROUND UP PROJECT ACTIVITIES

ACCESSIBILITY ADVISORY TEAM

The JMZ understood that growing its network of parents, service providers, and advocates in the disability community would be critical to providing knowledge and support for inclusion work. As the team crafted the AGU project activities—which included prototyping and building twenty-seven new exhibits, developing and testing a broad selection of accessibility supports and experiences, and intensive staff training and professional development—staff knew having a group of diverse and experienced advisers would be essential.

As the project kicked off, JMZ's accessibility coordinator—a new position funded by the grant—started reaching out to people in the disability community to invite them to join the advisory team. By the time the team's work began, it had grown to sixteen members, though the museum expected that not every member would be able to attend every meeting. Before the meetings commenced, the accessibility coordinator surveyed advisory team members to better understand their characteristics and participation preferences. This included questions about other disability organizations they were affiliated with, their current relationship with the JMZ, and what they expected to contribute to the collaboration. During the prototyping and testing phase of the project, an average of eight advisers attended each bi-monthly in-person meeting. Advisory team members were also available individually for specific consultation and advice as designers worked through challenges.

During the meetings, museum staff shared preliminary architectural and design plans for museum structural and exhibit elements, obtaining feedback, which they incorporated into the final designs. Advisers also tested exhibit prototypes and gave feedback on resources (such as tactile maps or sensory backpacks for use by children on the autism spectrum) as they were developed. In general, advisers responded favorably to prototypes and enjoyed seeing the process and sharing ideas. The exhibits staff incorporated most of their suggestions, though sometimes there were competing accessibility needs or a suggestion simply wasn't possible. In these cases, the group would talk through solutions or agree to compromise. Advisers indicated that they appreciated this aspect of the process because it helped them learn about other disabilities and why some designs may not be as inclusive as desired.

Outside of the meetings, the team experienced pushback from one exhibit designer who didn't fully embrace the task of incorporating the feedback and designing for accessibility in general. They felt it limited the visitor experience and required a lot of resources to provide access to a small portion of the museum's audience (e.g., Braille readers). Despite these reservations, unwavering institutional commitment to accessibility, staff training, and design support ensured this person's designs were accessible. For the future, the museum learned the lesson that hiring staff who embrace inclusive practices from the outset leads to a smoother team process.

STAFF TRAINING

To integrate inclusion deep into organizational practices, the museum needed to provide in-depth training on accessibility issues for staff and volunteers. The team started by conducting surveys to gauge their knowledge and find out what they wanted to learn. The needs and questions staff had varied by department. For example, the education department wanted to know what they legally needed to provide, like aides for students who needed support. The zoo department wanted to know about allowing service animals into animal areas. Staff in visitor services wanted to know about how to best interact with people with different disabilities. As the team looked through these responses, they came to realize that these unanswered questions were preventing staff from innovating beyond ADA minimums.

With support from our advisory team, the JMZ provided trainings that went beyond legal issues and gave staff and volunteers opportunities to understand the lives, challenges, and joys of children and adults with a variety of disabilities. As one JMZ staff member said, "I love how they [included] people with disabilities to help us understand what they do and go through. It really opened up a whole new insight for me." Some trainings consisted of hands-on sessions making support materials with Inclusion Collaborative, the accessibility arm of the Santa Clara County Office of Education. Others brought in speakers with disabilities and experts on childhood learning disabilities. With such a small staff, however, it was a challenge to get everyone to every training, as many had limited hours or pressing work duties. They creatively solved this by providing ten-to-fifteen-minute microtrainings at staff meetings to reach more people. The accessibility coordinator also developed a training program for onboarding new staff that is offered periodically. Facilitated by the accessibility coordinator, it includes a selection of online videos that feature people with disabilities so their perspective is represented.

JMZ's leadership team also attended two of the John F. Kennedy Center for the Performing Arts' Leadership Exchange in Arts and Disabilities (LEAD) conferences, which focus on accessibility issues in cultural centers. Through attending, the leadership team increased its working knowledge of accessibility issues and commitment to the project.

PROTOTYPING AND GATHERING FEEDBACK

To prototype new exhibits, experiences, and accessibility supports, the team turned to the Super Family Sunday events, which the museum continued to hold in JMZ's temporary facility during construction. These seventeen events—which were open to anyone who self-identified as benefitting from the format—included science activities and one-on-one time with zookeepers and animals for people of all ages with any disabilities. Super Family Sundays grew the JMZ family network, offered opportunities for formative and summative evaluation, and reinforced staff commitment to the project through firsthand experience with children with disabilities.

Super Family Sundays were useful because they set monthly deadlines to test new or tweaked prototypes with families. These prototypes were often rudimentary, and museum staff performed the evaluation in-house. Exhibit builders and designers casually observed people using the prototypes and asked questions to determine if the concepts made sense or visitors had suggestions or questions. Based on these observations, they decided whether to move forward with a design, make improvements for a future round of testing, or abandon the idea altogether. Some exhibits went through several rounds to finetune the user interface, while others had only one iteration. This informal approach worked for the small team and allowed for a nimbler process than a more structured evaluation. In the end, the team tested twenty-five exhibit prototypes at these events and with the general public.

Staff also conducted surveys at Super Family Sunday events to gather demographic information and feedback on visitors' preferences. They used this data both to make decisions about the events themselves, such as how many people to allow and what days and times to hold them, and to develop exhibits and access supports. For example, surveys asked attendees what specific types of fidget toys and other support items they would prefer for calming nooks and sensory backpacks. After learning conflicting information about sensory needs, the team decided to create two backpack prototypes to test, one for children with high sensory needs and one for children who benefit from calming items like noise reduction headphones.

Staff also conducted a few informal focus groups and special events with people who had specific disabilities to inform individual designs. For example, the museum invited the Vista Center for the Blind and Visually Impaired youth group to a special event where they tested audio and Braille labels. A group of parents of children with autism provided feedback on a scale model of our indoor calming nook and answered questions about ideal calming spaces. This approach kept the development process simple, within budget, and in motion.

THE NEW JMZ

The new JMZ facility, which opened in November 2021, nearly doubled the size of the old facility. It offers experiences that bring children nose-to-nose with animals, encourage imaginative play, support whole-body movement, and stimulate multiple senses. New JMZ attractions include an inclusive and wheelchair-accessible treehouse where kids can climb and explore at the heights of the birds and crawl through netted tubes above the zoo, providing a sense of what it's like to live in a canopy. The entire zoo is a netted aviary where birds and visitors roam freely together. More than fifty species of animals, from meerkats to raccoons, live among lush trees and shrubs, boulders, earthy nooks, and water elements.

Figure 3.2. A girl walks through the netted tubes above the zoo. She uses a motorized wheelchair to navigate the world. The elevator provided access to the treehouse and then she used the wheelchair transfer station to access the climbing nets. *Lisa Eriksen*

The new facility was intentionally designed to engage *every* child's curiosity in science and nature, and features a wide range of accessibility supports, including the following:

- Physical accessibility features (e.g., a wheelchair-accessible elevator to the treehouse, wheelchair transfer stations, benches with arms, places to hang canes, accessible parking, and accessible restrooms, including an adult-size changing table)
- Multisensory and accessible exhibits (e.g., exhibits explored through hearing, smell, and touch as well as sight; exhibits of varying heights for adults and children in wheelchairs; and exhibits with minimal reach ranges)
- Touchable, lifelike bronze sculptures of zoo animals
- Dedicated calming nooks in both the museum and zoo
- Accessible signage (featuring large print, high contrast, easy-to-read font, Braille titles, audio options, and tactile maps)
- Resources available for check-out (e.g., sensory support backpacks, noise canceling headphones, wheelchairs, large-print and Braille labels)

IMPACT ON FAMILIES WITH AND WITHOUT DISABILITIES

QUALITY OF THE EXPERIENCE

After reopening, external evaluator MWA Insights conducted summative evaluation to determine the impact of the accessibility work. The team collected data via postvisit surveys sent via e-mail to visitors who had reserved their tickets online. A total of 161 visitors who came to the JMZ during regular operating hours and sixty-one who came during Super Family Sundays completed the survey. The evaluator also conducted a series of focus groups with parents of children with a wide range of disabilities.[9] Overall, this research revealed that the new facility and ongoing Super Family Sunday events provided an exceptional experience for families with children with a disability. In several areas, the experience for these families was even better than that of families with no disabilities. As shown in figure 3.1, nearly 60 percent of families where a child had a disability rated their overall experience at the JMZ as "outstanding" compared to 41 percent where no family member had a disability. (However, it is worthwhile to note that most evaluation data from those with disabilities was collected from Super Family Sunday events, which do provide a different experience than a regular visit.)

Additionally, as shown in figure 3.2, families where a member had a disability were more likely to indicate that they felt welcome at the JMZ than families where no one had a disability. Both groups were equally likely to indicate that their family's needs were accommodated, that the level of the science content was appropriate, that their visit increased their interest in and understanding

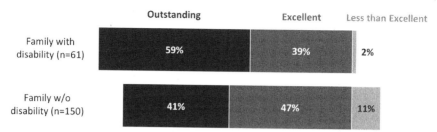

Figure 3.3. Ratings of visitors' overall experience at the Junior Museum & Zoo.
Lisa Eriksen, Tina Keegan and Maia Werner-Avidon

of science and the natural world, and that the ticket or membership price was reasonable—suggesting that the JMZ is providing an experience of similar quality to both audiences.

In focus groups, parents of children with disabilities also highlighted that they felt welcome and safe at the JMZ and that the experience had enhanced their children's science learning, particularly through the multisensory learning experiences and opportunities to get physically close to the animals and exhibits.

> I think that if this had been when [my son] was younger, just as a parent, to know that there were people who cared about [accessibility] would've meant a lot to me because it can be very isolating to have a disabled child . . . so that would've been huge for me to say, "Oh, my goodness, there's an entire museum looking out." That would've been huge. —Focus group participant

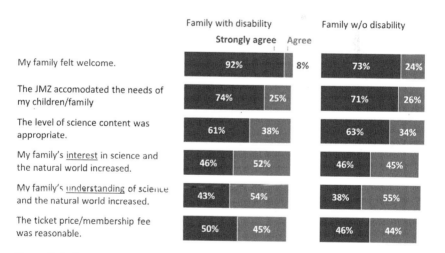

Figure 3.4. Percent of visitors who agreed with the following statements about their JMZ visit. *Lisa Eriksen, Tina Keegan and Maia Werner-Avidon*

I think it provided not just necessary supports, but enhanced supports. So that experience was like, "That was really cool," as opposed to, "Wow, I really struggled to get through that thing." . . . Our ongoing challenge is to find activities that are adapted enough and not overadapted, and I felt like it was a good fit for us." —Focus group participant

AWARENESS AND USE OF ACCESSIBILITY FEATURES

As seen in figure 3.3, survey results also showed that families with and without disabilities noticed and used the accessibility features at similar rates, suggesting that many of them have value for those outside of the disability community. One particularly interesting finding was that 70 percent of families where no one had a disability used the touchable bronze sculptures of zoo animals, compared to just over half of the families where a member had a disability.

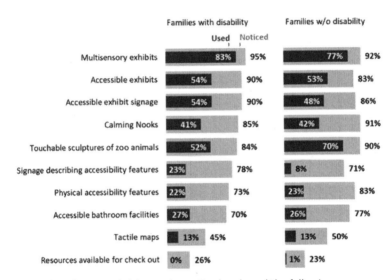

Figure 3.5. Percent of visitors who noticed and used the following accessibility features. *Lisa Eriksen, Tina Keegan and Maia Werner-Avidon*

Figure 3.6. A mom and her two children look at a realistic bronze raccoon sculpture which they can touch. The young girl has vision loss and is wearing dark sunglasses. She uses a cane to navigate. *Lisa Eriksen*

RAISING DISABILITY AWARENESS

In addition to providing a fully accessible experience to visitors with disabilities, the AGU project also sought to change the social experience for families with disabilities by raising awareness and increasing understanding among the broader community about the experiences of people with disabilities. As such, the JMZ team decided to call out various accessibility elements with signage to make them readily apparent to visitors both with and without disabilities.

Our survey also asked visitors about how their visit to JMZ impacted their awareness and perceptions of people with disabilities. Among families who did not have a member with a disability, many commented that seeing the various accessibility features (especially the adult-size changing table, calming nooks, and wheelchair elevator) and signage pointing them out increased their awareness of the challenges faced by people with disabilities and the tools available to help meet their needs. Some of their comments included the following:

> I was already aware of people with physical disabilities (I grew up in a house with a disabled sibling), but not as aware of people who need sensory breaks. This was very enlightening, and I was happy to see the quiet and safe spaces for them.

> The space for the adult changing table made me realize how frustrating it must be for someone who needs or benefits from that to have so little access.

> My son noticed the signs and I used this as a time to explain the needs for [people with] disabilities! Pretty informative and visual!

Families with and without disabilities both commented that the overall design of the facility showed them it was possible to seamlessly integrate accessibility features into a facility like this so that families with disabilities do not feel that they are being "othered":

> It's great to be a place that makes this accessible, so my child will see and understand that people with disabilities can take part and be a part of their experience, too. —Parent in family without a disability

> It seemed as though the museum's design incorporated their experience with those not considered disabled; in other words, it was part of our overall experience, not distinct or separate. —Parent in family without a disability

AN INCLUSIVE PROCESS AND AN INCLUSIVE FACILITY

Involving the disability community throughout the design process has led to a facility that is truly inclusive to children with disabilities. Taking time to have

Community Conversations, create an inclusion plan, regularly engage an advisory team, prototype exhibits, and conduct surveys and focus groups paid off in measurable successes. A nimble and ongoing evaluation process, both formal and informal, helped the JMZ to iterate and create an inclusive facility for all, as demonstrated by the summative evaluation.

Parents of children with disabilities said they felt welcome and safe at the JMZ and that the experience had enhanced their children's learning. At the same time, families without disabilities also had an enhanced experience thanks to the accessibility features, as evidenced by them using the features as much as (and in some cases more than) those with disabilities. The accessible design and explicit identification of accessibility features also enhanced disability awareness—and opened opportunities for conversation—among families where no one has a disability. This years-long process created a facility embraced and championed by families who have children with disabilities and fostered deeper connections to the community.

NOTES

1. Anonymous survey response from Junior Museum & Zoo Visitor, family with a child with a disability.
2. Anonymous survey response from Junior Museum & Zoo Visitor, family with a child with a disability.
3. Benjamin Zablotsky et al., "Prevalence and Trends of Developmental Disabilities among Children in the United States: 2009-2017." *Pediatrics* 144, no. 4 (2019): 3-5, http://publications.aap.org/pediatrics/article-pdf/144/4/e20190811/1332728/peds_20190811.pdf
4. Matthew J. Maenner et al. "Prevalence and Characteristics of Autism Spectrum Disorder among Children Aged 8 Years—Autism and Developmental Disabilities Monitoring Network, 11 sites, United States, 2020." *MMWR Surveillance Summaries* 72, no. 2 (2023): 4, http://dx.doi.org/10.15585/mmwr.ss7202a1
5. "Special Education-CalEdFacts," California Department of Education, accessed Sept. 20, 2023, https://www.cde.ca.gov/sp/se/sr/cefspeced.asp
6. Nicole Mlynaryk, "Autism Rates Continue to Rise in California," *Neuroscience News*, March 23, 2023, https://neurosciencenews.com/autism-california-22858/
7. Christine Reich et al. *Inclusion, Disabilities, and Informal Science Learning. A CAISE Inquiry Group Report* (Washington, DC: Center for Advancement of Informal Science Education, 2010), 11.
8. Reich, Price, Rubin and Steiner, *Inclusion, Disabilities, and Information Science Learning*, 10.
9. Evaluation also explored impacts on JMZ staff and advisory committee members. The full evaluation report can be found at: https://www.informalscience.org/access-ground-evaluation-report.

BIBLIOGRAPHY

California Department of Education. "Special Education – CalEdFacts." Accessed Sept. 20, 2023. https://www.cde.ca.gov/sp/se/sr/cefspeced.asp

Maenner, Matthew J., Zachary Warren, Ashley Robinson Williams, Esther Amoakohene, Amanda V. Bakian, Deborah A. Bilder, Maureen S. Durkin et al. "Prevalence and characteristics of autism spectrum disorder among children aged 8 years—Autism and Developmental Disabilities Monitoring Network, 11 sites, United States, 2020." *MMWR Surveillance Summaries* 72, no. 2 (2023): 1-14. http://dx.doi.org/10.15585/mmwr.ss7202a1

Mlynaryk, Nicole. "Autism Rates Continue to Rise in California." *Neuroscience News*, March 23, 2023. https://neurosciencenews.com/autism-california-22858/

Reich, Christine, Jeremy Price, Ellen Rubin, and Mary Ann Steiner. *Inclusion, Disabilities, and Informal Science Learning. A CAISE Inquiry Group Report.* Washington, DC: Center for Advancement of Informal Science Education, 2010.

Zablotsky, Benjamin, Lindsey I. Black, Matthew J. Maenner, Laura A. Schieve, Melissa L. Danielson, Rebecca H. Bitsko, Stephen J. Blumberg, Michael D. Kogan, and Coleen A. Boyle. "Prevalence and Trends of Developmental Disabilities among Children in the United States: 2009-2017." *Pediatrics* 144, no. 4 (2019): 1-11. http://publications.aap.org/pediatrics/article-pdf/144/4/e20190811/1332728/peds_20190811.pdf

4

Making History Accessible

EVALUATION AND STAKEHOLDER INVOLVEMENT IN THE EVOLUTION
OF AN ACCESS INITIATIVE

Charlotte J. Martin and Lynda Kennedy

WELCOMING ALL

Located at Pier 86 on the Hudson River in New York City, the Intrepid Museum is a nonprofit cultural and educational institution which illuminates the intersection of history and innovation through the people who lived it and the technology that made extraordinary accomplishments possible. To realize its core value of being welcoming and accessible to all, the museum has implemented many initiatives over the years to lower barriers, ranging from reduced and free entry to an investment in a variety of accessibility supports. These supports, which staff increasingly integrate into exhibitions and program offerings from initial design, have created an atmosphere where people with disabilities can feel welcomed as part of the expected and valued visitorship. Evaluation and stakeholder input has been essential to this work. Over the years, museum staff have employed surveys, observations, advisory groups, and user testing to measure success and inform future improvements. These efforts continue to evolve, as staff members seek to integrate accessibility and inclusion into all aspects of programming, exhibitions, interpretation, infrastructure, and visitor experience.

NEED FOR AND ORIGINS OF THE PROJECT

Centered on a landmarked aircraft carrier that served in the US Navy from 1943 to 1974, with collections including a submarine and a supersonic passenger jet Concorde, the Intrepid Museum is full of physical and sensory barriers to access due to the need to maintain the integrity of the landmark historic spaces. Regardless, when Intrepid staff began the institution's accessibility journey more than ten years ago, they began by asking "what can we do right now?" while planning for long-term work.

To determine where to start, the team began by considering the institution's strengths and seeking direct feedback from audiences. One definite strength was that "educating the public" was central to the museum's mission. Museum leadership had invested in its education team and prioritized programming that engaged both groups and individual learners, so it seemed like an obvious first step to expand on this by ensuring the programming was accessible to all learners. Already, education staff had seen the demand for this, as self-contained classes of students with developmental disabilities had begun booking guided school programs after the museum reopened in 2008 following an extensive renovation. Through conversations with teachers and colleagues, and, later on, through stakeholder surveys, the museum's educators learned more about the appeal of the museum for these groups. They created customized programs and approaches for these participants, providing visual vocabularies (key words illustrated with images) for programs, adding touch objects, incorporating physicality, which supported the concepts, and addressing the social-emotional goals of groups more specifically. In addition, the museum also began offering free tours either interpreted or led in American Sign Language (ASL), as well as verbal description and touch tours for both individuals and groups, increasing accessibility to adult and public education audiences.

Since these first forays, these initial programs have grown into a robust menu of specialized offerings and by-request programs, as well as public programs with inclusive accessibility baked in. In the process, a subsection of the education department has evolved into the access team, comprised of educators specially trained in providing supports for learners with disabilities. While originally it was only the access team who used these supports with self-contained classes of students with disabilities, the growing popularity of universal design and a move toward true inclusion in schools led educators throughout the department to begin including them in all of their programs. Using these resources is now standard practice at the museum, supporting learners with disabilities and those who learn best through different modalities. Likewise, staff members increasingly incorporate accessible communication methods, such as ASL and live captioning, into public programs as a regular best practice. The exhibitions team works with the access staff to meet and exceed standards set in the Americans with Disabilities Act (ADA) when designing new or updating existing exhibitions. The visitor services and security teams, who pride themselves on creating an excellent visitor experience, also work with the access team to integrate best practices for creating a welcoming and positive experience for those with disabilities into their regular team trainings.

THE ROLE OF EVALUATION AND STAKEHOLDER INVOLVEMENT IN THE PROJECT

Evaluation and stakeholder involvement have been essential to each step toward increasing accessibility at the Intrepid Museum. One of the best examples of this is the work staff members have done to evolve supports for people with autism. The team has used feedback not only to inform programming, but to evolve how and from whom feedback is solicited and incorporated. This began with an initial seed grant to develop sensory-friendly programming for children with autism and their families. The museum brought in the nonprofit consultant group Autism Friendly Spaces to conduct initial assessments, provide feedback on pilot programs, and help set up a parent advisory council. The council provided in-depth feedback on planned and past programs and later advised on the development of resources for all visitors, such as a general social narrative, a sensory guide and sensory kit, and a specialized maker camp for children with developmental disabilities. Access staff worked to ensure that the parent advisory council members represented the diversity of New York City, including primary language, cultural background, and professional status.

Several years ago, the team recognized that this group of advisers was not providing one important perspective: that of individuals with autism themselves. After hosting a focus group meeting for the museums, Arts and Culture Access Consortium's (MAC) Supporting Transitions project, to explore how cultural organizations can better support young adults with autism as they transition into adulthood, the museum's team decided to directly recruit adult self-advocates and rename the parent advisory council as the autism advisory council. In the intervening years, staff members have found that the adult self-advocates provide crucial insights that go beyond what the parent perspective can offer.

Initially, autism advisory council members who attended at least three out of four meetings and one program received a year of family membership in appreciation of their contributions. Additional funding now allows the museum to provide honoraria to council members in return for their participation. This way, we can acknowledge the expertise of our council members and help cover the costs of participating, such as transportation and childcare. We also updated recruitment materials and procedures for onboarding for new members. With the intended participants in mind, we created a flier that presents information in plain language and with corresponding visual cues, clearly outlining the goals and responsibilities of the council. We then began reaching to out to potential participants, sharing the opportunity with the MAC Supporting Transitions project—which by this point was also facilitating a self-advocate training program—and other local advocacy and service organizations like AHRC, an organization serving people with intellectual and developmental disabilities in New York City, and Felicity House, a free social community space for women

BOX 4.1.

Intrepid Museum Autism Advisory Council

The Intrepid Museum is looking for self-advocates to join its Autism Advisory Council for the 2023-2024 year!

The Autism Advisory Council:

- Discusses new exhibits and initiatives

- Gives feedback on Access Programs

- Talks about current concerns in their communities and shares resources

A good fit for the Autism Advisory Council is someone who is interested in cultural institutions and would like to join us in creating more accessible and inclusive spaces.

This recruitment flyer for the Museum's Autism Advisory Council clearly and accessibly describes the goals, requirements and rewards of participation.
Intrepid Museum

Autism Advisory Council Expectations:

 Attend at least 3 of 4 meetings a year. There will be two meetings in person at the Intrepid Museum and two meetings on Zoom.

 Meetings start at 6:00pm ET. Meetings at the Museum are 2 hours. Meetings on Zoom are 1.5 hours.

Autism Advisory Council Members will receive a $75 honorarium per meeting attended.

 Attend at least 1 Access program and provide detailed verbal or written feedback.

 Individuals that complete these expectations will also receive a year of Family Membership as a thank you for their participation.

For more information, please email Ellen Peiser at access@intrepidmuseum.org.

Intrepid Museum's Autism Advisory Council is generously supported by The Far Fund.

The FAR Fund

with autism. Access staff also approached participants in the museum's Sensory Friendly Evenings, wishing to have a mix of people both unfamiliar with and already invested in our programming, as we had done with our parent advisers. As a result of these changes and recruitment efforts, the museum brought on the largest proportion of new members yet, particularly self-advocates, but also parent advocates representing new constituencies.

To meet the needs of our participants, we established a few key practices from the outset. We committed to sending out agendas ahead of time, in plain language and with visual cues, to set expectations clearly and ensure that participants felt prepared. We made fidgets and noise-reduction headphones available and invited participants to move around or take breaks as needed. As the new council's work began, we made sure to gather feedback on how these practices were working and what else we needed to add. At the first meeting, for example, several self-advocates noted that they had a hard time following the discussion when topics strayed from the agenda or when the facilitators did not ask a specific question of advisers. Some also said fast-paced, overlapping conversation made it hard to keep track, particularly for those who prefer to communicate in writing. The access team took this feedback seriously and discussed how to update our protocols for the meetings. From there, we made several updates to our practices, including the following:

- Adding key questions under each section of the agenda we distributed in advance. This would give council members the opportunity to think about their feedback ahead of time and/or prepare themselves to participate at key points in the meeting.
- Reminding participants to stay on the agenda and offering to save time at the end of the meeting for additional discussion. We still wanted to allow for unanticipated points to come up, but not at the expense of allowing everyone to follow the meeting. Over Zoom, participants could also send chat messages to staff to share unrelated feedback or request discussion for later.
- For some questions, breaking into smaller groups, so that council members would have more room for participation. We divided parents and self-advocates between different staff, then shared a summary of the discussions when back together.
- Explicitly inviting and supporting different forms of communication. Both over Zoom and in person, we gave room for council members to share points in writing, in addition to verbally.
- Sharing information about any user testing ahead of time. For example, at one in-person meeting, we wanted feedback on virtual reality experiences and the mobile guide that the Intrepid Museum would be launching on Bloomberg Connects, a mobile platform hosting different museums and their collections. Council members knew what they would be testing ahead of time, so they had time to explore and, consequently, were able to give thoughtful feedback.

These updates have made for very productive and inclusive meetings. Both parents and self-advocates can participate in ways that work for them, and the access team can focus on the most pressing questions rather than simply reviewing recent programs. Throughout our first year of meetings, this receptivity and willingness to adapt has built trust with council members, making them more willing to share meaningful feedback. For example, even when some members became frustrated while user-testing the museum's Bloomberg Connects resource, they continued the exercise, trusting that we were taking their concerns seriously and that this was a worthwhile effort. Their feedback inspired important updates ahead of the museum's launch on the app, such as reorienting the app's map, clarifying its multilingual capabilities, and adjusting signage in the museum about what visitors can expect to learn from it.

The autism advisory council is just one of the ways the museum seeks feedback from audiences. We also collect it from access program participants with a range of disabilities and disabled user/experts we invite to test exhibit prototypes. We send follow-up surveys to school groups and other organizations that book guided programs. We encourage participants in Access Family Programs to complete surveys, both with QR codes posted in the activity space and follow-up emails within a day of the program. We update these surveys over time to address changing questions the staff has about the programs. For example, to get a better understanding of how some programs did or did not meet the social goals developed for family units with and without a disabled family member, we added questions about the extent to which the programs encouraged interaction with others within and outside of family units. This feedback helped museum staff make tweaks to the structured social opportunities (e.g., games or question prompt cards for guest experts) included in programs, and there has consequently been an increase in satisfaction reported in this area.

Participant and caregiver feedback is also important for more complex programs, like All Access Maker Camp, a weeklong program for children with developmental disabilities focused on problem solving, flexibility, socialization, and fun. The program's premise is that the campers' interest in the museum's content and in making, along with a highly supportive environment (i.e., trained staff, preprogram materials, visual supports, and adaptive tools), can motivate them to try things they might not otherwise attempt and build on their strengths in new ways. Parents and guardians receive postcamp surveys asking about the impact of the experience on the campers and their families, both during the session and in the period afterward. These surveys, which we have also adapted over time, collect a mix of quantitative and qualitative data. Responses to questions about specific interests or skills that campers continue to carry on after the camp experience have been important both for grant reporting and for informing changes in the program in subsequent editions. As we have continued to offer the program, surveys have also shown the clear impact of repeat participation for returning campers. Originally, we also hosted focus groups with parents after the camp had ended, but we did not continue this after the first year because we found the feedback was very similar to what we received in the survey, despite requiring more time, effort, and cost for both the participants and the museum. (Focus groups meant coordinating schedules and arranging for a facilitator and for educators to offer childcare.)

To capture a sense of the campers' direct experience, museum staff also created an observation rubric with indicators related to the main goals of the camp. These indicators encompass a wide range to reflect the diverse starting points and communication or behavioral characteristics of the campers. For example, the rubric lists nonverbal ways of responding to questions, such as pointing or using movements, and acknowledges that paying attention can look different for campers with disabilities. The range of indicators also addresses that campers are starting off at different points. The observation rubric has been used formally, but educators also use it informally at other times as a way to track camper participation over the week. The notes educators collect are helpful for the end-of-day educator debrief, so they can talk through approaches that are or are not working well, and then develop plans accordingly. They also inform the midweek reports we distribute to parents at pick-up on the Wednesday of each session, and overall feedback we provide them at the end of the session.

We applied a similar multipronged approach to evaluating our expanded Stories Within initiative, which consists of arts-based programming for individuals with dementia and their care partners. When we received additional funding from the Mellon Foundation in 2022 to expand both our onsite and offsite programs, we contracted with Museums Partners Consulting to develop surveys, observation rubrics, and interview protocols for both types of the programs. This combination of evaluative approaches has given greater insights into the program impacts than one approach alone.

After successfully expanding our accessible programming, the museum embraced a new goal: creating more accessible physical environments and interactive elements. To collect the necessary feedback from people with disabilities, staff members began employing prototypes, implementing user testing, and organizing focus groups. One example of this was the development of a semipermanent, accessible exhibition about the technology and history of the submarine *Growler*, which would bring immersive interpretation outside of the narrow and physically inaccessible vessel. This would achieve the twofold objective of expanding the stories the museum could tell about the crew and greater Cold War history than was possible inside the cramped spaces of the submarine itself, and to do so in a way that makes it accessible to all museum visitors.

For this exhibition, the planning team developed two interactive elements that enhanced the stories of submarine service with immersive features. One

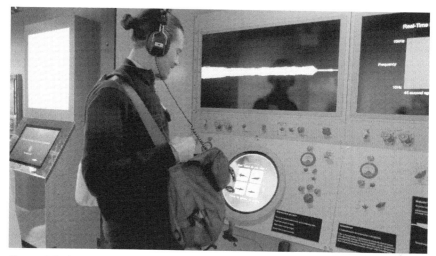

Figure 4.1. A visitor interacting with the sonar exhibit after installation. Sound waves are displayed on screen as the sound cues play in headphones and sound sticks.
Intrepid Museum

featured the sounds and vibrations of the submarine encountering different circumstances. The other focused on sonar, the tool which the submarine crew used to detect objects in the surrounding underwater environment by listening for signals. To develop and construct prototypes of both interactives, the exhibitions team partnered with the Stevens Institute of Technology. During the design process, we installed the prototypes in the museum's Space Shuttle Pavilion so that visitors could try them out while staff observed and asked questions, gathering meaningful feedback with ample time for the design team to make adjustments ahead of final installation. We also created an observation rubric and short survey addressing user experience and potential barriers.

These prototypes were open to all museum visitors during select times, but we also wanted to make sure to specifically invite disabled user/experts to give their detailed feedback, a practice modeled by the Institute for Human Centered Design (IHCD) and museums or museum projects like the Museum of Science, Boston, and Access Smithsonian. The access team reached out to local advocacy networks, such as the New York City chapter of the Hearing Loss Association of America, to local advocates of people who are blind or have low vision, and to members of the autism advisory council. Staff observers greeted the user/experts and brought them to each interactive exhibition prototype element. The observers made notes about how the user/experts explored the interactives and the barriers they encountered in use. Immediately afterward, the observers asked follow-up questions about the experience. This process proved very helpful. For example, feedback from d/Deaf user/experts helped develop the visualization component of the sonar interactive, where the audio is represented visually with animated sound waves. Those with low vision or limited dexterity gave important feedback on the user interfaces, such as the distribution of touch icons on the screen. Those in wheelchairs provided feedback on adjusting the vibration level. All of this user testing and the responses of the design team made for more effective and user-friendly interactives for all.

COLLABORATING WITH STAKEHOLDERS ACROSS INSTITUTIONS

Based on this accessibility work, the museum developed a larger national leadership project to create a digital toolkit that historic sites of all sizes could use to create their own accessible multisensory interpretation and exhibitions. Designing for accessibility can be particularly challenging for historic sites, which have to balance preserving spaces not originally built with accessibility in mind with serving and welcoming the public today. In addition to concerns about historic preservation, particularly for landmarked sites, many also have small staff sizes and budgets, making these efforts even more challenging.

In 2019, supported by an IMLS National Leadership Grant, the museum's team collaborated with New York University's (NYU) Ability Project to develop the sensory toolkit for interpreting historic sites, committing to making it free and accessible. The NYU Ability Project was the perfect partner because it is a joint research initiative with the occupational therapy department (NYU Steinhardt) and the interactive telecommunications program (NYU Tisch) that supports research in client-centered assistive technology and adaptive design for people with disabilities.[1] To support the work, the NYU Ability Project team planned a course during which students would develop prototypes designed to respond to the needs of specific historic sites and visitors with disabilities. Intrepid Museum's exhibitions team advised on the students' work and then further developed the prototypes. We installed the finished prototypes at the Intrepid Museum for initial user testing, and then other partner historic house and site museums created and installed their own versions for testing. The work culminated in the release of the toolkit.

The NYU Ability Project faculty and Intrepid's team shared a firm belief in the importance of including people with disabilities in all stages of the project. Advisers were also included from Access Smithsonian and the National Trust for Historic Preservation. Together, we opened recruitment for seven participating partner historic sites and a representative group of disability advocates. We created straightforward and accessible forms and included specific information about compensation and expected participation. We allocated funds to paying disability advocates honoraria at different stages of the project in recognition of their time and expertise. Staff members from the partner historic site museums would have travel costs covered and their institutions would receive funds to support the prototype development and user testing. To make our toolkit as applicable to a wide range of museums as

Charlotte J. Martin and Lynda Kennedy

possible, it was important that the sites reflected a diversity of types, budgets, staff sizes, history of accessibility efforts, and geography. For the recruitment of the disability advocates, the aim was to assemble a group who could represent and provide insights on experiences of those with physical, sensory, and cognitive disabilities. We created simple application forms for each group and shared these widely. Our advisers and partners were crucial in helping with this recruitment and in reviewing the applications.

The full group convened in December 2019 to identify the priority areas for the project and make sure that everyone understood their responsibilities throughout the process. To make sure the meeting would be accessible for all contributors, we took the following steps:

- Sending detailed agendas, slides, and introductory materials ahead of time
- Ensuring all materials were screen-reader-accessible (i.e., proper formatting of documents and alt text for all images)
- Budgeting and arranging for live captioning (CART)
- Making sure museum staff were prepared to greet people at the museum entrance and assist with wayfinding
- Assisting with accessible arrangements for those traveling
- Requiring all meeting attendees to use a microphone when speaking to the whole group
- Having designated notetakers so we could send notes afterward
- Having noise reduction headphones and fidgets available at all times
- Using a mix of large-group and breakout-group discussions
- Making sure the concluding dinner (the only offsite event) was at an accessible restaurant

In addition to these preparations for the structure of the meeting, the project team also thought about what should be accomplished in the content of the discussion. A key objective was defining what was meant by "accessible sensory interpretation." The full group agreed our work would not be about meeting the basics of ADA compliance; rather it would be about addressing how historic sites make their stories more accessible and meaningful to more people through multisensory design and engagement. We would consider how sites can creatively and affordably remove communication and information barriers, while involving people with disabilities in the process. Coming to this shared understanding enabled the group to identify the three main barriers for consideration during the project:

1. Things behind glass: For preservation and safety reasons, historic sites and museums may need to keep certain areas and artifacts behind a barrier, thus physically separating visitors from opportunities to engage with them beyond one specific view.

2. Over- and understimulating environments: Some areas in historic sites and museums, especially those with outdoor components, may be overwhelming for some visitors, with excessive noise, smell, heat/cold, or visual stimuli. Others may not be stimulating enough, lacking opportunities to engage with multiple senses and form different connections with content.
3. Spaces that are closed to everyone: Many historic sites have areas they cannot open to visitors at all for safety and preservation reasons, as the Intrepid Museum does with certain sections of the ship. However, these nonpublic spaces are also part of the site's story and have valuable information to convey if this barrier can be overcome.

The next stages of the project focused on the development of prototype solutions to address these challenges. The team worked to plan the evaluation of these prototypes for their effectiveness, accessibility, and feasibility for others to implement. The toolkit would then share the findings and provide resources and case studies for readers at other historic sites and museums. To ensure the toolkit would be meaningful, evaluation in varying forms was necessary at all stages of the project, including reflective evaluations on the project team's interactions and convenings.

In winter 2020, NYU Ability Project convened its class for the project, with members of the Intrepid Museum's team, disability advocates, and partner historic site representatives joining throughout the semester to describe their challenges, ask and answer questions, and provide feedback as students started their projects. The historic site representatives had an incentive to participate because they could clarify their needs and guide students as they worked, potentially improving experiences at their sites, while disability advocates could help ensure that their concerns were factored into designs from the beginning. The students worked on the projects in groups, with each selecting one of the general challenges we had identified to address. During classes, they had the opportunity to meet with project stakeholders to share updates, and they also documented their progress on a class website.

Like many activities in 2020, the project was disrupted by the COVID-19 public health emergency beginning in March. As an immediate impact, the NYU class shifted to a virtual platform, and students lost access to the campus buildings and labs they would normally have been able to use to develop prototypes. Students continued their work despite this, developing digital approaches or detailing plans for physical prototypes—though without the ability to fully implement and test their designs. At the end of the semester, they presented their work to stakeholders, who joined virtual class presentations and/or reviewed the presentation materials. The historic house and disability advisers completed a simple survey on each project.

Though the project continued during the pandemic, it faced serious disruptions, including the inability to create full student prototypes, furloughs and

Charlotte J. Martin and Lynda Kennedy

layoffs at some historic house museums, and the fact that the Intrepid Museum remained closed through summer 2020. This led the project leaders to seek an extension from IMLS and postpone the prototype exhibition by another year. As a bonus, this would also allow NYU Ability Project to run the class a second time, with new students able to learn from the previous students' projects as they developed their own approaches. The historic house and site museums would also have time to bring back staff from furlough or reassign the work. (One site dropped out of the project after laying off its accessibility staff, while another reassigned a new staff member to work on the project after laying off its original representative.)

The Intrepid Museum and Ability Project also used the delay as an opportunity to collaborate on another project to address new needs presented by the pandemic: how to prevent crowding around exhibit labels and replace physical shared audio guides. We collaborated on a digital project to create a template and process to develop an affordable, flexible, and easy-to-update mobile guide that other historic house museums could easily replicate and update for themselves. As part of this project, the museum created an inventory for the first time to streamline the decades of existing but disparate content on exhibit labels, the outgoing audio guide, our YouTube channel, and an audio description and tactile guide with a talking pen supporting visitors who are blind or have low vision. The mobile guide we produced also incorporated wayfinding directions to supplement the museum's map and address challenges to navigating a historic ship. Faculty and students on the NYU Ability Project team designed a basic mobile-first site on WordPress, working with the museum's web team to make sure it was easy to update and maintain. The museum's curatorial and access teams prepared and updated content and ensured that all media, including photos and videos, were accessible, with updated image descriptions for alt text and captioning and descriptions for videos. Ahead of reopening, the museum worked to ensure awareness of the guide's availability, creating new large-wall labels with QR codes linking to it, as well as adding links in ticket confirmation emails and on the museum's website.

Again, evaluation was essential to this undertaking at all stages. For this project, the team worked closely with one of the disability advocates, Cheryl Fogle-Hatch, who advises on museum and digital accessibility. She is blind and uses a text-to-voice screen reader on computers and mobile devices. In addition, Lauren Race of NYU Ability Project conducted remote user testing and interviews with members of the museum's autism advisory council, the museum's older volunteers, and others before the museum reopened to the public. Testers visited the mobile site from home and commented as they used it, with Lauren asking follow-up questions throughout. These interviews informed tweaks to wayfinding and the included content information. Once the museum reopened to visitors, Lauren and others from NYU Ability Project conducted observations on several weekend days at the museum to see how visitors accessed the guide, which led to recommendations on the location of QR codes. This work culminated in a journal article[2] and also laid the foundation for one of the projects explored by the NYU class in winter 2021. This early feedback, as well as later visitor feedback, helped inform the museum's approach to adopting the Bloomberg Connects platform in summer 2023, including increasing the amount of audio content (rather than primarily digital text).

In January 2021, the historic houses and museums, disability advocates, advisers, and project leads reconvened over Zoom to ensure that all stakeholders were ready for the next steps and NYU Ability Project could make adjustments to their course curriculum as needed. Participants reflected on changes to their work and needs since the start of the pandemic. Intrepid Museum and NYU Ability Project representatives shared information about the accessible mobile guide and the projects from the previous year that students in the new class would follow up on. The class started soon after—this time over Zoom from the beginning, but with students able to meet in person and access NYU's labs and resources. Historic site representatives and disability advocates joined classes when able, meeting with groups working on projects of interest. For example, the representative from Fort Ticonderoga (in Ticonderoga, New York) met frequently with the student group working on the accessible mobile guide, the representatives from Macculloch Hall Historical Museum (in Morristown, New Jersey) and Louisiana State Museum (in New Orleans, Louisiana) met with students and Intrepid Museum staff working on creating tactiles for objects and artworks behind glass, and the representative from Bainbridge Island Historical Museum (on Bainbridge Island, Washington) met with those exploring olfactory (scent-based) experiences and ways of incorporating multiple narratives into a space. As with the previous year's class, the students presented their progress midway through the semester and at the end, with historic sites and disability advocates providing feedback through a simple survey for each group.

Feedback on the final presentations and throughout the semester informed the plans for *Making History Accessible*, a temporary exhibition at the Intrepid Museum showcasing prototypes conceived and created by both the NYU students and the Intrepid Museum exhibitions team, as well as context about the project and disability in historic houses and museums generally. The featured projects included the following:

- A tactile partial recreation of a historic stove that is up steps and behind a barrier in a museum, with audio interpretation from a multiple perspectives
- A toolkit to support the use of plain language in labels and descriptions, with examples written and recorded for an artifact in the Intrepid Museum's collection
- Tactile versions of historic portraits of George Washington developed by a student, showcasing the use of simple inexpensive materials and the iterative process

Figure 4.2. The temporary exhibition *Making History Accessible* displayed the prototypes developed by NYU Ability Project and the Intrepid Museum's Exhibitions team in a prominent area of the Museum. *Intrepid Museum*

- Accessible mobile guide templates
- Raised line texture for historic photographs paired with scent jars, designed to keep the smells contained and be easy to replenish

The museum and NYU Ability Project took a multipronged approach to evaluating the prototypes in the exhibition. The avenues for feedback included public surveys, user/expert testing with observations and interviews, and feedback from disability advocates and historic sites at the fall 2021 convening. To recruit participants for the public surveys, the museum set up a kiosk near the exhibition with the survey available both on mounted tablets and on paper. The museum's information desk staff were also prepared with an easy system for visitors to request to take the survey verbally, with a museum staff member or volunteer recording their answers. The survey asked about visitors' engagement with the various prototypes and how effective they were. Questions were mostly quantitative (using rating scales) with room for open-ended feedback, should a visitor be interested in sharing any. The multiple formats were meant to make it easy for any visitor to share feedback, though a major limitation was that the information about the survey was available only in English.

As with the Intrepid Museum's previous testing of the submarine exhibition prototypes, we sought more in-depth feedback from those who most typically face barriers in historic sites. Advisers at Access Smithsonian provided valuable support as we instituted the protocol for this process. For recruiting, we contacted existing disability networks and asked our disability advocates to share the opportunity widely. Museum and NYU Ability Project staff conducted testing during designated times, going one-on-one (or one-on-family, if a family came together) with user/experts through the exhibition, recording observations on a rubric: Where did the user go first? Where did they get stuck? How much time did they spend with different elements? We asked clarifying questions so that user/experts did not have to try to remember or retain everything that they did, or every hiccup that they encountered, which is especially important for someone who struggles with working memory. Afterward, the staff person conducted a brief interview based on the survey in a quiet area of the museum. We invited user/experts to stay in the museum afterward, if they wished, and also gave them two free passes to the museum for a return visit.

These layers of feedback provided important findings ahead of the fall convening of historic sites and disability advocates. For example, user/expert observations and feedback made clear how important the ability to turn off audio would be. One person with autism and sensitivity to noise found the audio disruptive and distressing to be unable to turn off. Others just wanted to be able to move on or try something else. Visitors who were blind or had low vision provided key feedback on the tactile stove reproduction, noting that the partial design, nonmetallic materials, and lack of a full model for scale limited their ability to access information and context about the relevance of the installation. Meanwhile, the almost evenly split survey responses around preference for the plain language or more technical versions of labels helped us better recognize the need to provide information to visitors in layers, so they can get a foundation of basic information and proceed to more technical details as they choose.

When the full project working group convened in person with a Zoom option in October 2021, historic sites and disability advocates got to experience these prototypes for themselves (or watch others do so) and hear the full findings from the Intrepid Museum team. They had the opportunity to ask questions about the processes and costs (a major concern for all museums, but especially those with small budgets and staff) and to brainstorm ideas for potential partners and vendors in their own communities. Representatives from each site then selected a prototype to create and install in their own locations. By the following summer they would provide the findings from their own evaluation, based on the existing survey and interview instruments. Each site received a modest stipend to support the work and receive continued advisement from the project team.

The site prototyping stage was essential to the evaluation of this project, as the implementation at the diverse sites would provide a proof of concept

Charlotte J. Martin and Lynda Kennedy

for anything put into the final toolkit. To what extent were the processes and resources useful for different historic sites, and what had we missed, if anything? Did the sites have the resources they needed to identify and work with local stakeholders?

The findings from the historic sites and their evaluations would greatly inform the suggestions and resources that made it into the final public toolkit. For example, Eastern State Penitentiary (in Philadelphia) worked with a vendor to create a full tactile model of its historic prison building using 3D printing, learning a lot about the appropriate level of detail through multiple iterations along the way. The Louisiana State Museum took the feedback about the historic stove in the Intrepid Museum's exhibition and sought out a local vendor to develop an improved version that could be installed in an accessible location near the actual historic stove. After one vendor fell through due to cost, museum staff found a new one who was excited about the challenge and worked closely with them to decide where it was important to emphasize detail in 3D and where they could reduce costs by using less detail with flat photos. Rather than the textured flat version at the Intrepid Museum, they built out a full three-dimensional version with aluminum casts of the iron to maintain the shape and texture of the original. They also incorporated an iron kettle and scent jars, collecting feedback from visitors with disabilities to hone these features. Meanwhile, Fort Ticonderoga rolled out and updated its accessible mobile guide, testing it out through the vast outdoor site, and incorporated layers of information for a wide variety of visitors.

Throughout the process, Intrepid Museum and NYU Ability Project staff were available to the historic sites to provide feedback and support. The team then incorporated these communications, as well as the sites' reports from onsite evaluation, while creating the toolkit during the summer of 2022. To ensure the toolkit's clarity and usefulness, we continued to rely on user feedback throughout the writing process. Once the first draft was completed, we shared it with the project advisers, historic sites, and disability advocates for their responses and suggestions, as the final component of their contributions to the project. The toolkit had to make sense and meet the needs of these constituencies. Their feedback contributed to major revisions, which included a more robust appendix of case studies and resources, sample evaluation instruments, and suggestions of disability advocacy organizations with local chapters around the country. The final version, *Making History Accessible: Toolkit for Multisensory Interpretation*, is now available on the Intrepid Museum's website as a jumping off point for any historic sites or advocates interested in this work.[3]

CONTINUING THE WORK

As we continue to work toward a more accessible and inclusive museum, evaluation efforts at the Intrepid Museum increasingly engage self-advocates throughout the process of exhibition and program development, as well as work on historic spaces. Building on our work with the autism advisory council, and with self-advocates on the sensory tools project and exhibit prototyping, the museum team has secured funding to compensate additional advisers and user/experts for their time and expertise in the feedback process. New areas of focus include plans for an updated education center, virtual reality experiences for areas fully inaccessible for all visitors such as the ship's engine room, and plans to open a large area of Intrepid to the public for the first time. The last project will involve interpreting the ship's historic sick bay, both within and outside of the physical space, with hands-on and digital interventions. All projects will have disabled user/expert input and feedback. In addition, the museum recently redesigned its website, contracting the Institute for Human Centered Design to provide guidance and feedback throughout the development process, including from its team of web accessibility experts and pool of disabled user/experts.

The museum has maintained its relationship with the NYU Ability Project, with staff members advising on student work or presenting exhibition design challenges as part of coursework. Several students have pursued this work in greater depth, focusing their thesis projects on developing novel approaches to creating meaningful tactile replicas. The museum supports their endeavors by making collections available to them and providing a space for testing and feedback from visitors. One of these students explored different potential ways of creating meaningful tactile versions of crew patches in the Intrepid Museum's collections.[4] She developed several prototypes from different materials and with different means of incorporating description. She and her adviser brought these to the museum on several occasions, with support from the museum, and invited visitors to try them and share feedback. She experimented with mechanical embroidery on heavy paper to create simplified reproductions of patch designs, so that the tactiles used the same materials (thread) as the originals. She also worked closely with blind designers for feedback. The museum is now able to use these designs in programs and potentially in future exhibitions.

Accessibility work, especially at historic houses and museums, is always a work in progress. At the Intrepid Museum, basic evaluation work helped kickstart efforts and has only continued to enrich the work as we engage more deeply and regularly with our diverse disability communities.

NOTES

1. "An Interdisciplinary Research Space Dedicated to the Intersection of Disability and Technology." NYU Ability Project. Accessed November 17, 2023. https://wp.nyu.edu/ability/.
2. Race, Lauren, Charlotte Martin, Xinwen Xu, Cheryl Fogle Hatch, and Amy Hurst. 2021. "Bring Your Own (Accessible) Device: A Mobile Guide Solution for Pro-

Charlotte J. Martin and Lynda Kennedy

moting Accessibility, Social Distancing, and Autonomy in Museums." *The International Journal of the Inclusive Museum* 15 (2): 1-23. doi:10.18848/1835-2014/CGP /v15i02/1-23.
3. *Making History Accessible: Toolkit for Multisensory Interpretation* is available for free download as a PDF or Word Doc at https://intrepidmuseum.org/resources /accessibility-tools.
4. Koseff, Stefanie. Tactile interpretations of historical embroidered patches, 2023. https://www.stefaniekoseff.com/recent-research/tactile-interpretations-of-historical-embroidered-patches/.

BIBLIOGRAPHY

Koseff, Stefanie. Tactile interpretations of historical embroidered patches, 2023. https://www.stefaniekoseff.com/recent-research/tactile-interpretations-of-historical-embroidered-patches/.

NYU Ability Project. "An Interdisciplinary Research Space Dedicated to the Intersection of Disability and Technology." Accessed November 17, 2023. https://wp.nyu.edu /ability/.

Race, Lauren, Charlotte Martin, Xinwen Xu, Cheryl Fogle Hatch, and Amy Hurst. 2021. "Bring Your Own (Accessible) Device: A Mobile Guide Solution for Promoting Accessibility, Social Distancing, and Autonomy in Museums." *The International Journal of the Inclusive Museum* 15 (2): 1–23. doi:10.18848/1835-2014/CGP/v15i02/1-23.

5

Integrating Formative Accessibility Testing into Evaluation for an Immersive STEM Exhibition

Elizabeth Kunz Kollmann, Leigh Ann Mesiti Caulfield, and Tim Porter

The Museum of Science, Boston (MOS), has a long history of leveraging research and evaluation to inform decision-making about our products and practices—particularly those related to exhibitions. As far back as the 1970s, MOS began to collect data about our visitors to understand the kinds of content that might be attractive to them as well as how they were using exhibition components. Research and evaluation became more formalized at the museum in the late 1980s and early 1990s, when MOS worked with George Hein and his team at Lesley University to conduct evaluations of our "Science is an Activity" exhibitions, such as *Investigate!*[1] and *Seeing the Unseen.*[2] Reports about these projects describe some of our first forays into formative evaluation, where the Lesley University team provided data to help us think about changes that we might want to make to individual components or entire exhibition spaces, and summative evaluation, where data allowed us to better understand overall exhibition and component use as well as what visitors could learn from their exhibition experiences.

Because of this and other evaluation work being conducted around this time, including studies conducted by Dr. Betty Davidson, which will be described later in this chapter, there was an increased interest in evaluation within the Museum of Science as a way to improve exhibition experiences for visitors. Therefore, in the early 2000s, some MOS staff formed a group known as the Marketing, Exhibits, and Programs Evaluation and Research Committee. This group crafted protocols for allowing outside researchers to conduct research and evaluation at MOS, as well as conducting some evaluation studies of its own. As this work continued, the museum finally decided in 2004 to form an internal research and evaluation department, with Dr. Christine Reich as the founding manager. By this point, staff had come to feel that formative evaluation was critical to their exhibition development process, and that there needed to be staff dedicated to this work. In the years since, the research and evaluation department has grown to ten staff members who conduct more than thirty research and evaluation studies for the museum each year. Our work covers a range of topics and kinds of educational deliverables, and we conduct front-end, formative, remedial, and summative studies for MOS.

THE BEGINNINGS OF ACCESSIBILITY EVALUATION AT MOS

At around the same time that George Hein was conducting some of the first MOS formative and summative exhibition evaluations, Larry Bell and Betty Davidson pursued and received a grant from the National Science Foundation (NSF) to improve the accessibility of the museum's New England Wildlife Zones exhibition. The New England Wildlife Zones exhibition, which would later become New England Habitats, consisted of a series of dioramas displaying taxidermied wild animals from New England surrounded by murals of their natural habitats.[3] Unfortunately, because these dioramas were housed behind glass, they were not very accessible. The research project, led by Dr. Davidson, set out to add components to this space to increase its accessibility for those with a range of disabilities, including those who are blind or have low vision, who have limited mobility, and/or who are d/Deaf or hard of hearing.

The New England Habitats NSF project and resulting revised exhibition were a turning point for the Museum of Science. It was through this work that MOS explored the use of multimodal exhibit components, adding elements that allowed visitors to touch, hear, and even smell exhibits, so that sight was not the only sense they were using to interact with the exhibits. Staff added these sensory elements at multiple locations throughout the space so that visitors could continue to interact in the way that they were most comfortable as they progressed through the exhibition. For example, they added smell boxes to all of the dioramas so that visitors could smell the animals and their habitats. Staff added Hearphones—which provide exhibit content, instructions, and verbal description through physical, hand-held speakers—so that visitors could listen to labels instead of having to read them. They also added taxidermy and bronze casts of animals to the space so that visitors could feel the animals instead of only being able to look at them. Through the research, staff found that creating multimodal experiences like these led to better learning outcomes for everyone, not only those who had disabilities.[4]

This project was also the first time that MOS did formative accessibility testing with visitors with disabilities. For this research, staff invited people with disabilities to experience early versions of exhibit components while they observed them and asked them questions about their experiences. Staff also asked them to take part in focus groups to give feedback about the direction that the new space was taking. Finally, staff brought in accessibility consultants to help the team think about their design decisions. From this project, MOS learned lessons about improving our development process and visitor outcomes that we continue to apply in our exhibition design today.

CASE STUDY: THE *ARCTIC ADVENTURE: EXPLORING WITH TECHNOLOGY* EXHIBITION

The rest of this chapter will discuss the development of *Arctic Adventure: Exploring with Technology*, with a focus on the formative accessibility testing that we used. This exhibition opened at the Museum of Science in December 2020.

Arctic Adventure: Exploring with Technology, otherwise known as *Arctic Adventure,* is designed to invite visitors to explore an immersive Arctic environment via a mixed physical and digital setting, with the primary intended message that we can use technology to explore our environment and identify problems we need to solve. The exhibition has several educational and experiential goals, which are listed in box 5.1.

BOX 5.1. *ARCTIC ADVENTURE* EXHIBITION GOALS

Educational Goals

- Visitors will learn about a *range of technologies* that can be used to make observations about the environment they are in.
- Visitors will identify the *constraints and affordances* of different technologies.
- Visitors will *explore* a given technology to learn the extent of its capabilities and usefulness.

Experience Goals

- Visitors will feel as though they have been transported to an Arctic environment.
- Visitors will be curious about the environment they are in.
- Visitors will use technology to explore the exhibition's Arctic environment.
- Visitors will feel that there is something new to explore each time they visit.

Figure 5.1. The Entrance for the *Arctic Adventure* exhibition was designed to evoke that this would be an immersive experience. © *Museum of Science*

This exhibition is composed of six areas, each of which was designed to be immersive and accessible. These are the areas:

- "Entryway": This section is filled with elements that immerse visitors in the Arctic environment and introduce them to some of the technologies and species they will encounter across the exhibition. It includes multiple touchable elements, including a real ice wall, examples of the technologies that visitors can expect to investigate across the exhibition, and bronze replicas of species that are seen across the exhibition experiences. Additionally, there is a soundscape designed specifically for the exhibition that begins in the entryway with a video of a fox making sounds such as scratching and squealing.
- "Ice Core Drilling": This section explores the drilling tools that researchers use to extract ice cores. Visitors can manipulate an interactive hand auger and larger ice core rig and watch or listen to a captioned large-scale video that explains the tools and processes by which we derive ice cores in the Arctic, enabling scientists to better understand climate change.
- "Hydrophones": This activity uses a floor-projected ocean scene, showing a range of Arctic aquatic species swimming in the water underfoot. On two sides of this projected floor are stations that introduce visitors to hydrophones, a technology that researchers use to capture the soundscape under the Arctic ice. These interactive stations allow visitors to use this technology to listen for evidence of underwater animal sounds and identify the animals that created them. An accompanying spectrogram enables visitors to also "see" the sounds, a multimodal aspect that helps everyone and makes the component accessible to those who are D/deaf or hard of hearing.

- "Arctic Vista" (drones and global positioning system [GPS] activities): This area is a sprawling digital Arctic landscape populated with a host of terrestrial and aquatic species. The activity invites the public to send virtual drones out into the vista to survey the landscape, and to explore GPS data of other species. This section includes touchable physical models of drones, bronze ivory gulls with GPS tracker "backpacks," and a real polar bear GPS collar.
- "Ice Core Theater": This immersive theater evokes what it might feel like to step inside a glacier, surrounded by a series of illuminated ice cores. The light in these cores is synchronized to the floor-to-ceiling media presentation telling the story of climate change across our planet and how that story has been formed through the data derived by examination of hundreds of thousands of years of data found in layers of ice.
- "Navigate": In this collaborative, interactive experience, visitors are challenged to safely traverse a glacier while retrieving lost supplies by using a combination of ground penetrating radar (GPR) and satellite data. The simulated glacier is created via a combination of physical and dynamic digital elements and stretches across the exhibit floor. Visitors work in pairs, using a hands-on GPR scanner to find and avoid hidden "crevasses" across a floor-projected ice sheet and satellite data to help them locate supplies. If a visitor steps on a hidden crevasse, a projected image dramatically shows a gaping hole beneath their feet, and their supplies "fall" into the virtual crevasse. This activity employs visual, sonic, and haptic elements and is adjoined by a real example of a GPR device and case.

To ensure that all visitors could physically interact with the space, cognitively engage with materials, and socially interact with one another, the design team applied universal design and universal design for learning principles to the development of the exhibition. Universal design (UD) is a set of principles developed by architecture professionals for optimizing the accessibility and usability of a physical space.[5] Universal design for learning (UDL) is a set of principles developed by educators from the research and development organization CAST for the design of learning experiences. The UDL framework suggests providing multiple means of engagement, representation, action, and expression to increase accessible learning experiences for a range of learners.[6] In applying UD and UDL principles to this exhibition, the MOS team hoped *Arctic Adventure* would be usable and understandable by the widest range of people operating in the widest range of situations, without the need for special or separate accommodations.

THE ARCTIC ADVENTURE TEAM AND DEVELOPMENT PROCESS

Creating a permanent exhibition at the Museum of Science often takes many years, and *Arctic Adventure* was no different. The development process began in 2017, three years before the exhibition opened in 2020. Beginning phases of the development involved testing exhibition concepts with different museum audiences, including general visitors, MOS members, and educators. Once the concept had been decided upon, the team began brainstorming components for the exhibition, which we then prototyped and refined to arrive at a decision about the final activities for the space. Then, the exhibition went into the production phase. When *Arctic Adventure* opened, the team conducted a remedial process to address any issues we uncovered. Due to the highly digital nature of this exhibition, the remedial process was the first time some activities were prototyped with all of the technology installed.

It took a whole team of exhibit professionals to develop this exhibition. A project manager made sure that the project moved forward on time and on budget. Content developers defined the educational goals, messages, and stories the exhibition needed to convey, and brainstormed with the exhibit designers and interactive media designers about how to bring them to life through physically and digitally based experiences. The exhibit designers and interactive media developers then designed and constructed those components, doing their best to ensure that they would be accessible to a broad range of visitors. We also worked with an external partner, Moment Factory, a multimedia entertainment studio that specializes in the creation of immersive environments. Moment Factory applied its digital and storytelling expertise to this exhibition so that all components would tell key stories across a large-scale, tech-integrated environment. Finally, evaluators were a part of this team across the span of the project, helping the team think through the goals of the exhibition and determine when it would be best to use evaluation to get public feedback on ideas or prototypes. We also made sure to collect data about the accessibility of components throughout the development process, including perspectives from visitors with disabilities.

PLANNING HOW TO MAKE ARCTIC ADVENTURE ACCESSIBLE

Conducting formative accessibility testing is an important part of the MOS exhibition development process. With the emphasis on *Arctic Adventure* as a universally designed, immersive environment, formative accessibility testing was particularly critical. While evaluators performed typical formative accessibility testing tasks, like consulting with our external accessibility advisory committee and inviting people with a range of disabilities to participate in accessibility testing, we also added other steps to the process for *Arctic Adventure*, like creating UD plans for each of the exhibition components and making use of user personas.

One of the first steps in the formative accessibility testing process for *Arctic Adventure* was using these personas, or fictionalized individuals, to think about the experience that visitors with a range of disabilities might have using different components within the exhibition. We used eight different personas to represent potential user or visitor types, which were based on many years of formative accessibility evaluation with visitors with disabilities[7] (see box 5.2).

BOX 5.2. MOS VISITORS WITH DISABILITIES PERSONAS

Based on previously collected formative accessibility data, MOS created eight visitor-with-disability personas. These were the personas:

1. Ron: A thirty-four-year-old adult with low vision who is expert in using computers and has a strong interest in science. He visits MOS when we have new offerings, attending with a friend who helps him navigate the space.
2. Cynthia: A fifty-six-year-old adult who became blind as an adult. She uses technologies like computers but would not consider herself an expert. She knows basic science and attended the MOS more often when she had young children. When she does visit, she comes with her husband and daughter.
3. Addison: A thirteen-year-old girl who is Deaf. She uses the internet to play games and interact with friends. She takes science classes in school but sometimes struggles with them. She visits MOS with her family often. This group includes her parents and siblings.
4. Allan: A seventy-one-year-old adult who has hearing loss but does not consider himself to have a disability. He doesn't use computers very often, but he loves science and volunteers at MOS. Beyond volunteering, he also visits MOS with his grandchildren. He uses hearing aids while at the museum to support his hearing.
5. Mimi: A forty-seven-year-old adult who has multiple sclerosis, causing her to use a power scooter. She is not an advanced computer user. She has a science background through the high school courses she took and her experiences at MOS. She visits MOS and other museums often with her husband and son.
6. Molly: A twenty-seven-year-old adult with an intellectual disability. She is comfortable with basic computer use and doesn't particularly like science. She visits the museum about once a year with the other residents and staff from her assisted living center.
7. Alec: A twenty-five-year-old male with autism spectrum disorder. He is comfortable with computers and likes the idea of science, although he has had difficulty learning it in the past. He visits MOS often with his mother but prefers visiting art museums.
8. Cameron: A sixteen-year-old male who does not consider himself to have a disability. He uses computers to play games, watch videos, and do social networking. He enjoys math and chemistry. He visits MOS with his grandmother and sister.

We repurposed these personas from an earlier Museum of Science project called Creating Museum Media for Everyone (CMME)[8], which also involved making a range of media and technology interactions accessible.

Using these personas, the *Arctic Adventure* team discussed each profile in relation to each of the exhibit components, as well as to the exhibition overall. By having individuals that we could refer to when thinking about the range of abilities and interests of potential visitors, the team could start considering the aspects of the design and content that might or might not work well for visitors with disabilities. This process helped us revise design ideas even before prototype creation.

To illustrate how this process works, here are examples of how we used two of our personas: Ron and Molly. The Ron persona is an adult with low vision who visits MOS with friends who can help him navigate the space. Because of this, we concluded that Ron might not enjoy visiting *Arctic Adventure* if the space was too busy and too loud. We began to discuss how we could make the space auditorily appealing and ensure that content could be heard as well as seen. We also discussed how we could make the space bright enough that it could be easily navigated by a visitor with low vision. Finally, the Ron persona encouraged the team to consider how to best communicate where pieces of the exhibits are located, like the GPR scanner for "Navigate."

The Molly persona has an intellectual disability. She visits the museum with other residents from her assisted living center and is comfortable with basic computer use. We concluded that the *Arctic Adventure* space with its digital aspects would probably be appealing to Molly. However, because processing information takes her more time, she would need clear, simple instructions for interactives. We would also want to make sure that digital activities, like "Hydrophones" and the "Arctic Vista," did not time out too quickly.

Based on these personas and on other team member expertise, the evaluators and *Arctic Adventure* team created UD plans for each of the exhibit areas, identifying accessible features or considerations we thought should be a part of the exhibition. Each of these UD plans described the visitor goals for the space and the universal design elements that could be included for successful interaction. The UD elements section described aspects of the content, audio, mechanical interactives, software, video and AV, graphics, artifacts/objects, and social interactions that would contribute to the accessibility of the component. Box 5.3 shares the UD elements that were in consideration for the "Entryway" area.

The UD plan was also a place where the team could document questions or concerns that we had about the accessibility of an exhibit component. For example, in the "Arctic Vista" and "Hydrophones" space, the team was concerned that if the space was too bright, it might be difficult for visitors with low vision to read text on the exhibit labels and touchscreens. We also had questions about how to make touchscreens navigable for visitors who are blind

BOX 5.3. "ENTRYWAY" UNIVERSAL DESIGN ELEMENTS

MOS created universal design plans for each exhibit component as a way to think through potential accessibility issues and how they might be addressed. The information below is the plan for addressing accessibility as a part of the *Arctic Adventure* "Entryway."

Content

- The goals for the exhibition are presented.
- It is clear to the visitor they are entering a new environment.
- Simple, audience appropriate language is used.
- Multiple people, teams, roles in the Arctic are presented.

Artifacts/Objects

- Physical objects or interactives reflect the *Arctic Adventure* theme and provide context for exhibit experiences, such as:
  - Pelican cases with looping media of Arctic animals and researchers in the field
  - Touchable physical objects like an ice wall, cold weather gear fabric samples, and/or a model of bird with a tracking backpack
  - Objects that humanize the environment, such as a rock climber mannequin

Graphics

- A main title, paragraph, and/or question are included.
- The primary message is introduced.
- Supporting graphics include text and pictures to contextualize how the artifacts are used in the real environment.

Audio

- Sounds of wind, ice crunching underfoot, and ice cracking are included to place visitors in the Arctic environment.
- Audio labels accompany the video/AV elements, with caption and/or printed text.

(continued)

Mechanical Interactives

- The physical elements are an appropriate height and are accessible for young children or those using wheelchairs or canes.
- Adequate lighting/projections are provided for those who are low vision.

Software

- Any software elements incorporate a clear layout, font, color, and graphics, including action items located on bottom third of screen.
- There is an option for visitors to choose audio for text instructions.

Video and AV

- There is environmental imagery and video of Arctic environments, animals, and research with minimal text.
- Video and AV includes appropriate lighting.

Socially Interact with One Another

- There are atmospheric/environmental cues (e.g., ice crunching underfoot, touchable ice wall) that surprise and evoke groups.

and how to program them so that they did not time out on those who needed more processing time, without frustrating visitors who needed less processing time. Finally, the team wondered if it would make the "Hydrophone" component more inclusive to visitors who were d/Deaf and hard of hearing if we added visual spectrograms. By documenting these concerns early in the development process, evaluators were able to focus their data collection on these questions during the formative evaluation testing.

Once the team completed these planning processes, it was time to start creating and testing exhibit prototypes. The next section will describe the formative evaluation process in greater detail, including how we involved visitors with disabilities and accessibility experts.

Figure 5.2. Visitors using the "Arctic Vista" component where UD and accessibility testing was especially important to the screen and lighting design. © *Ashley McCabe*

Figure 5.3. Visitors exploring the "Hydrophones" component where spectrograms were added based on formative accessibility testing to compliment audio components. © *Nicolaus Czarnecki*

FORMATIVE TESTING TO MAKE *ARCTIC ADVENTURE* ACCESSIBLE: THE "NAVIGATE" EXHIBIT EXAMPLE

Formative evaluation was an important part of *Arctic Adventure's* development process, particularly for the "Navigate" activity, which entails physical and digital interactions along with complex partner collaboration between visitors. To prototype this component, the exhibit team tested early concepts to explore potential activity dynamics. We designated a large space of the museum floor to serve as a crevasse-filled ice field, rolling out paper versions of crevasses and giving testers low-tech props, such as dowels with paper plates on the end to simulate holding a GPR scanner. Content developers then gave the testers verbal commands as to where it was safe or unsafe to walk across the landscape. This exercise helped the exhibit team try out different activity instructions and understand visitors' first instincts of how to interact when confronted with this chaotic activity. From this testing, we concluded that we should build a secondary goal into the activity, beyond simply traversing the Arctic environment while avoiding crevasses.

"Navigate" testing then graduated to a hybrid physical and digital experience, where the exhibit team projected a crevasse-dotted landscape on the floor that was manually operated by keyboard commands. (This is sometimes referred to as "Wizard of Oz" testing, meaning visitors experience what feels like automated interactivity, but a staff member is actually controlling the exhibit manually while observing their actions.) The team laid out a large white canvas cloth as the activity gameboard and gave visitors metal detectors to hold in place of the GPR scanner. We tested and iterated this version of the activity multiple times to advance our thinking around activity dynamics, usability, and content learning. This stage of formative evaluation explored several questions, such as these:

- How might visitors engage with this activity solo?
- If "Navigate" were a partner activity, how could we provide two roles that give visitors both meaningful and engaging experiences?
- How could we make both roles accessible to a range of audiences?
- What instruction and content supports would we need to provide for all visitors to successfully engage?
- How could we ensure the activity was both fun and accurately represented how scientists might use crevasse detecting technology to explore an Arctic environment?

We were still conducting formative testing with our general visitors during this phase, but this was also the point in the process when we began our focused formative accessibility testing with visitors with disabilities.

Figure 5.4. Visitors prototyping an early version of the "Navigate" component where the MOS team learned that it was important to add a visitor goal to the activity. © *Museum of Science*

Given the prevalence of temporary and permanent disability, which is estimated at 20 percent of the global population at any given point,[9] evaluation with general visitors can help to uncover accessibility barriers and supports on its own. At the Museum of Science, approximately 11 percent of visitor groups report having someone in their group with a disability.[10] However, there are times when targeted recruitment and testing with visitors with disabilities can be called for, such as during formative evaluation, when the team is testing exhibits with a small number of groups, often in a short amount of time. This way, we can uncover accessibility issues early enough in the process for teams to transform those needs and preferences into purposeful exhibit design. The goal of formative evaluation is to identify and prioritize the most urgent educational, interest-related, and usability information, which is why holding space for visitors with disabilities during this development stage can provide key insights into how best to transform universal design principles into practice.

For our formative evaluation of *Arctic Adventure,* we recruited visitors with disabilities primarily through the museum's exhibit accessibility testing database, which evaluators began many years ago as formative accessibility testing needs at MOS increased. To build it, evaluators reached out to organizations and individuals to find people with disabilities who were interested in being a part of our accessibility testing. The list, which we regularly update throughout the year, includes contact information for families with at least one person who identifies as having a disability, as well as community groups that serve individuals with disabilities who are interested in bringing a group in for testing. It also includes information on each individual's disability type and requested accommodations, as well as background information, such as age, gender, last date of visit, group size, and interests. When participants from the list come into the museum for a testing session, we compensate them for their time and feedback with gift cards from American Express or VISA. We also give them and their group free admission and parking at the museum on the day of testing.

One large-scale effort in our formative accessibility testing took place in June 2019, when the full exhibit team, including both MOS and Moment Factory team members, hosted a two-day evaluation charette at the museum. During this charette, the team set up the "Navigate" and "Drones" activities in one of the museum's theater spaces, where MOS staff, general visitors, a community group, and visitors with disabilities participated in testing. Because Moment Factory's team was onsite, they temporarily installed technologies for "Navigate" that we had not been able to test in our "Wizard of Oz" scenario, including a computer vision technology called OptiTrack for object tracking and LiDAR technology that could digitally detect where people were on the ice field. The team was considering these technologies for use in the final version of the component, so testing them afforded us both visitor data and technology feasibility data. This weekend of testing provided a valuable, eye-opening experience for all team members, as we were able to observe

BOX 5.4. TIPS AND TRICKS FOR FORMATIVE ACCESSIBILITY TESTING

1. Make sure to plan for accessibility testing far ahead of time. The steps listed below all take time, and in particular, you may need weeks or even months to recruit testing participants. So, make sure to plan for accessibility testing early and give project teams a heads up that they need to add in extra time to their development timeline for formative accessibility testing.

2. Think about what your evaluation questions are and which audiences might be able to best answer those questions. If you are wondering about whether buttons are reachable or too difficult to manipulate, you may want to recruit visitors with mobility issues. If you are concerned that your exhibit or environment is too stimulating, you may want to recruit visitors who are neurodiverse.

3. Reach out to local schools and organizations who serve the individuals with disabilities that you are hoping to test with. They may be willing to reach out to their members to see if anyone is interested in testing out exhibits or may want to bring in a group for testing themselves.

4. Provide compensation for visitors with disabilities who come in for accessibility testing. Besides providing free admission to your museum, think about what other barriers you may want to lower. Can you provide transportation or at least reimbursement for visitors' travel? Can you provide a gift card to visitors for giving their time and expertise?

individuals interacting in real time with our designs and speak with them first-hand about their needs and preferences for this exhibit. Through observing visitors, particularly those with disabilities, we saw our design choices and their implications made real. This testing also provided an opportunity for us to troubleshoot potential design solutions together with visitors, elevating the visitor's voice during the design process.

Another way that the *Arctic Adventure* team elicited feedback from people with disabilities was through the museum's external accessibility advisory committee. This group consists of individuals from the Boston community who both identify as having a disability and have expertise working with and for people with disabilities as part of their careers. The museum meets with this committee up to two times a year to discuss accessibility strategies and challenges for exhibits in varying stages of development and compensates them for their time. For *Arctic Adventure*, this committee reviewed early concept drawings of the exhibition and discussed how the museum could incorporate potential multisensory aspects to ensure a universally designed exhibit for all. One of the central questions for the committee related to how to make "Navigate" a successful partner and/or solo activity for visitors. They helped us envision supports that would help the trekker, who was navigating the ice field, and navigator, who was helping the trekker to avoid the crevasses, better communicate with one another. Once *Arctic Adventure* was open to the public, the accessibility advisory committee visited and shared feedback on how well we had integrated certain accessibility features, if we should pursue any further changes to the exhibition, and what lessons we might consider for designing future exhibits.

Through our testing with visitors with disabilities and feedback from the accessibility advisory committee, we made the following changes to "Navigate" to make it more universally designed for audiences with a range of abilities and disabilities:

- Adjusting the minimum distance between crevasses so that visitors with assistive technologies, such as wheelchairs or seeing-eye dogs, would not accidentally open a crevasse while looking for missing supplies.
- Determining the optimal height and handle design for the GPR tool so that people who use wheelchairs or have limited dexterity could use it. The team set the height low enough that someone in a wheelchair could easily push it in front of or beside them and chose a T-shaped handle design suitable for different types of grips.
- Adding multiple signals to alert the trekker to hidden crevasses. This included vibrations for haptic feedback and increased color contrast between the crevasses and background, based on feedback from visitors who were blind or had low vision, and a red-green colored light signal on the base of the GPR, based on feedback from visitors who were d/Deaf or hard of hearing.
- Developing a whimsical video label to describe the premise of the activity and roles of each partner, rather than relying on only written instructions. We captioned the video so visitors could read along and also shared the instructions over broadcast audio for visitors who might not be able to see the video or read the text.
- Using LiDAR technology to allow the navigator to see the location of the trekker in real time on a digital kiosk map as they led them to missing supplies. This eases the difficulty of interpreting the map, a particular concern for those with cognitive disabilities, and it eliminates the need to split attention between the ice field and map.

Figure 5.5. Visitors using the final version of the "Navigate" component with the accessible GPR scanner. © *Nicolaus Czarnecki*

FINAL OUTCOMES FOR VISITORS

After the museum completed the *Arctic Adventure* exhibition and opened it to the public, the evaluation team conducted a summative evaluation to understand whether we achieved our goals for the exhibition.[11] In particular, we wanted to explore how the immersive and UD elements that we included in the exhibition supported or hindered visitor outcomes, both for general visitors and for visitors with disabilities. We used random sampling to generate our general visitor sample but recruited visitors with disabilities through our exhibit accessibility testing database. To understand how these two groups interacted with the exhibition and what impacts it had on them, we observed what components they visited and the behaviors they displayed at them. We also interviewed and surveyed them to understand their perceptions of the exhibition and the elements of the experience that helped or hindered accessibility. To help you think about accessibility elements that you might want to include in your own work, we are sharing a short summary of the findings from the summative evaluation in the following paragraphs.

When asked how they felt about *Arctic Adventure*, both general audience visitors and visitors with disabilities reported they had positive experiences in the space. Both groups cited many of the UD features of the exhibition as elements that made it memorable and interesting. These included touchable artifacts like the ice wall and bronze casts of Arctic animals, the digital projections like those that were part of the "Vista" component, and sensory components like the soundscape. For example, one visitor said, "I like the real ice. I felt like I was actually in the Arctic."

We also asked both groups about the elements within the exhibition that contributed to the cognitive, social, and physical accessibility of the space. Both general audience visitors and visitors with disabilities said that roleplaying as a researcher and being immersed in the world of Arctic Adventure aided in their learning. For example, one visitor said, "Switching roles was fun. I really felt what I was doing was important." They also reported that multimodal aspects of the exhibition, such as the text labels, audio, and video, helped to make it cognitively accessible. Visitors reported that enabling them to watch other visitors engage in activities and including activities that required collaboration with others promoted social accessibility in the exhibition. For some, however, these collaborative activities were actually a deterrent to social accessibility, when they did not have a partner to collaborate with. One visitor said, "There was a person in front of us trying to do the activity by herself, and [she] didn't know how to work ["Navigate"] by herself." Aspects of the exhibition that aided physical accessibility included having ample space to navigate, seats for resting, and closed captioning. Some visitors reported that physical accessibility was impeded by quiet auditory components that they could not hear. One of these visitors said, "The volume was a little low, so we either had to hold [our child] or use the step stool if she wanted to see or hear."

LESSONS LEARNED BY THE ARCTIC ADVENTURE TEAM

Throughout the Arctic Adventure development process, the exhibit team witnessed the value of prototyping early and often, even when early versions were low-tech concept prototypes or manually controlled "Wizard of Oz" testing. For "Navigate," we had to creatively problem solve early on, designing prototypes with enough scale to give visitors a sense of what the activity would be like in its final design, but enough agility that we could change elements and avoid investing upfront in technology we might not end up using. One advantage of this approach was that it helped us define our intended activity flow and the supports visitors would need *before* adding the complexity of new technology. We used findings from visitor testing, particularly accessibility testing, to articulate exactly how we needed the high-tech elements to function for the exhibit to be successful. One disadvantage, however, was that we could not troubleshoot and calibrate the technology until remedial testing. There were elements of how it behaved in the busy, real-world museum space, particularly its accuracy in detecting people and objects in space, that could not be replicated until the final install.

One struggle that the exhibit team encountered during *Arctic Adventure's* development was balancing our desire for authenticity with our desire to include meaningful multisensory supports. To be true to the science, we wanted to be as authentic as possible in how we showcased Arctic technology in the exhibits, but at times this authenticity conflicted with multisensory accessibility needs. In the end, we deferred to including the UD supports to create more engaging and accessible visitor experiences. For example, while a real explorer using a hydrophone in the Arctic primarily relies on audio cues to understand which animals are in the water below them, in the "Hydrophones" activity we decided to add spectrograms to the kiosk screen to illustrate the broadcast audio sound waves as an image. This helped visitors who were d/Deaf or hard of hearing to successfully engage with this activity, and it created a better experience for general visitors as well, who may have a visual preference or trouble hearing the audio in a particularly loud exhibition space.

The exhibition area that included the "Arctic Vista" (drones and GPS) and "Hydrophones" activities was a challenging section for the team to develop overall. Because the two activities rely on different sensory cues (sound in "Hydrophones" and visuals in the "Arctic Vista") to achieve the same purpose of finding animals, we originally intended for visitors to learn the same things from engaging with either one. For that reason, we determined that it was acceptable for one of the components to include mostly visual interaction and the other mostly auditory, so that visitors with hearing or sight differences could access at least one. However, we learned in the remedial and summative evaluations that visitors did not feel that these activities were equivalent and felt that they were missing out on content if they could only interact with one of the activities and not the other. In the end, adding audio description overviews and audio layers to the data presented in the "Arctic Vista" activities did not create an analogous experience for someone who is blind and did not allow someone who is blind to successfully engage in the intended activities. This affirmed for us that it is best, when creating a truly accessible exhibit, to make every activity as multimodal as possible.

Another challenge involved audio labels, which we use to provide content, instructions, and verbal descriptions to a range of audiences, including visitors who are blind or low vision, are early learners and prereaders, or have learning disabilities such as dyslexia. In the past, we used Hearphones for this purpose, which had been the primary method for delivering auditory information across the museum. But because Hearphones required visitors to hold a physical speaker up to their faces, they became a safety concern during the COVID-19 pandemic. To minimize the spread of transmission at a time of heightened concern, the museum removed Hearphones from all existing exhibits and specified that new exhibits would need to incorporate broadcast audio and/or connect with an audio app (which was still in prototype form).

Broadcast audio was an effective way to deliver the audio content, but a disadvantage of this strategy was that it added more sound to an already loud exhibition, and at times made it challenging for visitors to adequately hear the audio in different areas. This is a challenge that the museum will continue to address as we develop future exhibits.

While creating exhibitions that integrate physical and digital elements was not new for the museum's exhibit developers, the scale of this integration and level of immersion in *Arctic Adventure* was a new and exciting challenge. To accomplish this, the museum team knew we needed a partner who had demonstrated technical expertise in digital and physical world- building and could leverage this expertise to create an immersive space where visitors could accessibly interact and learn. Working with the team at Moment Factory helped the museum translate its vision for an exhibition about Arctic technology into a magical space that felt different than any other at the museum. Moment Factory brought ideas about technology and immersion that we did not have previous experience with, such as the LiDAR technology we used to track visitor movement in the "Navigate" activity. In return, Moment Factory learned how to integrate educational goals into an exhibit experience, which it had not done before, in focusing almost exclusively on user experience. Our relationship also helped Moment Factory to think about the accessibility of an experience in a more holistic way, including integrating UD and UDL principles more than they had ever before. Finally, while Moment Factory had some experience with user testing in previous projects, participating in the design charrette exposed them to a much deeper and more multifaceted form of evaluation and helped them think about how they may integrate it into their future work.

The integration of physical and digital elements in the exhibition created a rewarding experience for visitors but required the team to make difficult choices and think creatively about design. Our commitment to universal design and universal design for learning throughout the process has evolved our thinking about what accessibility can look like for high-tech, informal learning spaces, and we hope it can do the same for the broader field. Achieving these results would not have been possible if not for the robust and extensive formative accessibility testing that we undertook during the exhibition design process.

ACKNOWLEDGEMENTS

Without the work and support of many MOS staff, the *Arctic Adventure* exhibition would not have been possible. Thank you to members of the exhibit team for their work developing the exhibition, including Lindsay Bartholomew, Sara Castellucci, Jessica Ghelichi, Mike Horvath, Nora Nagle, Bobbie Oakley, Alana Parkes, and Ben Wilson from the Museum of Science, and Cloe St-Cyr, Amahl Hazelton, and David Conway from Moment Factory. Thank you to members of the research and evaluation team, including Allison Anderson, Keith Allison,

Karri Folks, and Sunewan Paneto, who worked on the formative and summative evaluation for this project. Finally, thank you to the Institute for Museum and Library Services (IMLS; MA-10-19-0206-19) for providing funding for the development and evaluation of this exhibition.

NOTES

1. George E. Hein, Judith Kelley, Elsa Bailey, and Kerry Bronnenkant, *Investigate! 1996 Summative Evaluation Report*. Cambridge, MA: Lesley College Program Evaluation and Research Group, 1996.
2. George Hein and Susan Cohen, *Seeing the Unseen An Exhibit of Boston's Museum of Science Interim Formative Evaluation Report*. Cambridge, MA: Lesley College Program Evaluation and Research Group, 1992.
3. "Making Natural History Exhibits Multi-Sensory; Improving Learning for Disabled Visitors," NSF Award Abstract, Accessed September 11, 2023, https://www.nsf.gov/awardsearch/showAward?AWD_ID=8652311&HistoricalAwards=false
4. Betty Davidson, Candace Lee Heald, and George Hein, "Increased Exhibit Accessibility through Multisensory Interaction," *Curator* 34, no. 4 (1991): 273–90.
5. Bettye Rose Connell, Mike Jones, Ron Mace, Jim Mueller, Abir Mullick, Elaine Ostroff, Jon Sanford, Ed Steinfeld, Molly Story, and Gregg Vanderheiden. "The Principles of Universal Design: Version 2.0." Last modified April 1997, https://design.ncsu.edu/wp-content/uploads/2022/11/principles-of-universal-design.pdf
6. David Rose and Anne Meyer, *Teaching Every Student in the Digital Age: Universal Design for Learning* (Alexandria, VA: Association for Supervision and Curriculum Development, 2002).
7. Stephanie Iacovelli, "Using Personas in the Design Process of Digital Exhibit Interactives." Last modified July 2014, https://www.openexhibits.org/paper/using-personas-in-the-design-process-of-digital-exhibit-interactives/
8. "Creating Museum Media for Everyone," Open Exhibits, accessed September 11, 2023, https://www.openexhibits.org/research/cmme/
9. Lise Wagner, "Disabled People in the World: Facts and Figures," accessed September 11, 2023, https://www.inclusivecitymaker.com/disabled-people-in-the-world-in-2021-facts-and-figures/; Lise Wagner, "Invisible Disabilities: 80% of Disabled People Are Concerned!," accessed September 11, 2023, https://www.inclusivecitymaker.com/invisible-disabilities-80-of-disabled-people-are-concerned/
10. Alexander Lussenhop, "Collaboration for Ongoing Visitor Experience Studies Museum of Science 2022 Data Summary" (presentation Museum of Science Culturally Responsive Programming and Equitable Access Committee, Boston, MA, April 2023).
11. Sunewan Paneto, Karri Folks, and Elizabeth Kunz Kollmann, *Arctic Adventure Summative Evaluation Report*. Boston: Museum of Science, 2023.

BIBLIOGRAPHY

Connell, Bettye Rose, Mike Jones, Ron Mace, Jim Mueller, Abir Mullick, Elaine Ostroff, Jon Sanford, Ed Steinfeld, Molly Story, and Gregg Vanderheiden. "The Principles of

Universal Design: Version 2.0." Last modified April 1997, https://design.ncsu.edu/wp-content/uploads/2022/11/principles-of-universal-design.pdf

"Creating Museum Media for Everyone." Open Exhibits, accessed September 11, 2023, https://www.openexhibits.org/research/cmme/

Davidson, Betty, Candace Lee Heald, and George Hein. "Increased Exhibit Accessibility through Multisensory Interaction." *Curator* 34, no. 4 (1991): 273–90.

Hein, George, and Susan Cohen. *Seeing the Unseen An Exhibit of Boston's Museum of Science Interim Formative Evaluation Report*. Cambridge, MA: Lesley College Program Evaluation and Research Group, 1992.

Hein, George E., Judith Kelley, Elsa Bailey, and Kerry Bronnenkant. *Investigate! 1996 Summative Evaluation Report*. Cambridge, MA: Lesley College Program Evaluation and Research Group, 1996.

Iacovelli, Stephanie. "Using Personas in the Design Process of Digital Exhibit Interactives." Last modified July 2014, https://www.openexhibits.org/paper/using-personas-in-the-design-process-of-digital-exhibit-interactives/

Lussenhop, Alexander. "Collaboration for Ongoing Visitor Experience Studies Museum of Science 2022 Data Summary" (presentation Museum of Science Culturally Responsive Programming and Equitable Access Committee, Boston, MA, April 2023).

"Making Natural History Exhibits Multi-Sensory; Improving Learning for Disabled Visitors." NSF Award Abstract, Accessed September 11, 2023, https://www.nsf.gov/awardsearch/showAward?AWD_ID=8652311&HistoricalAwards=false

Paneto, Sunewan, Karri Folks, and Elizabeth Kunz Kollmann. *Arctic Adventure Summative Evaluation Report*. Boston, MA: Museum of Science, 2023.

Rose, David, and Anne Meyer. *Teaching Every Student in the Digital Age: Universal Design for Learning* (Alexandria, VA: Association for Supervision and Curriculum Development, 2002).

Wagner, Lise. "Disabled People in the World: Facts and Figures," accessed September 11, 2023, https://www.inclusivecitymaker.com/disabled-people-in-the-world-in-2021-facts-and-figures/

Wagner, Lise. "Invisible Disabilities: 80% of Disabled People Are Concerned!," accessed September 11, 2023, https://www.inclusivecitymaker.com/invisible-disabilities-80-of-disabled-people-are-concerned/

6

An Iterative Approach to Accessibility

TRANSFORMING MUSEUM PROCESS WITH EXPERIMENTATION
AND EVALUATION

Sarah Schleuning

speechless: different by design was an experiment—a museum exhibition that in its making involved seven artists-designers, an evaluator, nine scientists and researchers, multiple consultants, two museums, dozens of staff members, and the generous support of donors, foundations, and sponsors.[1] Its intent was to foster inclusion, empathy, and a greater understanding of how we experience the world through our varied senses, merging research, aesthetics, and innovative new design. The entire project championed open-ended thinking and iterative approaches to develop greater investment from staff, leadership, and the communities we serve as well as reinforce the notion that innovative accessibility work requires constant dialogue, experimentation, and feedback.

Art has the power to change people's lives in positive ways, and after decades as a curator, I wanted to find new ways to connect to people who don't interact with the visual in "standard" ways. speechless explored diverse ways of interacting with art that diverge from the usual ways of experiencing a museum exhibition—attending a show, viewing artworks (without touching them), reading labels, and listening to audio guides. Knowing that everyone learns in different ways, and that the museum's visiting public is not a monolith, we wanted to offer new works in a presentation that challenged those traditional paradigms.

The project had four distinct components:

1. The exhibition, on display at the Dallas Museum of Art (DMA) from 10 November 2019 to 13 March 2020, was co-organized by the DMA and High Museum of Art.[2]

2. The catalog, *speechless: different by design* (2020) documented the research and development of the exhibition.[3]
3. The Visitor Research Study (VRS)—developed by independent evaluator Azucena Verdín, PhD,[4] in consultation with me—was an evaluation of the exhibition to gauge its reception.
4. *different by design: the speechless project*, the electronic publication published the following year, reported out the exhibition's evaluation, impact, lessons learned, and next steps.

Though the exhibition and catalog were typical outputs of museum experimentation, the evaluation and follow-up publication were less so—but equally important. As a foundational and scientific evaluation, the VRS provided substantive feedback and analysis on the relationship between visitors' sensory differences and their social and emotional responses in the installation. This helped us encourage a more iterative approach to accessibility at the DMA and in the broader field going forward, as we used the findings to start a larger discussion amongst stakeholders and then shared them with a wider audience through *different by design*. This assessment of our findings, like all elements of the process, eschewed a formal, closed-doors approach in favor of inviting the public into the experience by disclosing the challenges we faced and reflecting on lessons learned. This chapter includes many elements and components, condensed and revised, of that report.[5]

The experimental nature of *speechless* offered fertile ground—a rich and provocative learning experience in the making, the viewing, and the reflection. It broke new ground for what a museum exhibition can be. This embrace of experimentation made our evaluation work especially helpful. By taking the time to evaluate, we could better understand what it takes to be an expansive and inclusive environment in which to experience art, and then capitalize on this information to further explore ways we could innovate toward that objective.

In our evaluation, we had an impressive 82 percent positive rating from our visitors. Additionally, the show garnered extensive positive media coverage, including in national outlets such as *PBS NewsHour*, *Forbes*, and features in two AAM blog postings.[6] *Forbes* called it "A new exhibition that bucks the status quo . . . broadening the idea of visual communication." *The New York Times* declared the installations "cutting-edge works." *The Dallas Observer* described the show as "a vast immersive sensory experience." And *The Dallas Morning News* proclaimed, in a front-page story, that "in the age of . . . pop-up entertainment venues, whose only function is to provide a backdrop for the self-indulgent vanity shot, the DMA show aims to do precisely the opposite: arouse empathy."

EMPATHY AT THE CORE

The origins of *speechless* are connected to my own experience with my children. My son Vaughn, now ten years old, has a neurological motor-planning condition that makes speech difficult, and was nearly nonverbal for the first several years of his life. This led my family to adapt to different methods of communicating, to become much more aware of the range of ways in which we process sensory information, and to develop an expanded consciousness, appreciation, and empathy for how people with neurological differences experience the world and how the world responds to them. As a result, I began to question the potential role of art, museums, and museum exhibitions in the lives of people with neurological differences.

Because empathy had inspired the exhibition from its conception, it became interwoven as a theme in the research and development, a central focus for the artists-designers, scientists and specialists, and evaluator from the outset.

For the VRS evaluation, empathy became the key query in the framework our consultant, Verdín, developed. Verdín and I began discussing the project when she was on DMA's staff as an evaluator focusing on general visitor surveys. Though she left the museum during the planning of the show, we were able to contract her to continue to build the framework, oversee conducting the evaluations, and produce the final report. Her deep knowledge of the institution's visitorship, fluency with the scholarship on the science of evaluations, and shared experience parenting neurodivergent children made her an ideal partner. We worked closely together, challenging each other to think holistically yet keep the scope measurable.

One of the areas we discussed in depth was in what capacity we could measure empathy. After extensive conversations during the lead-up to the exhibition, Verdín helped explain the challenges of measuring changes in a visitor's empathy levels as a result of engaging with the art in a museum setting:

> When you have a concept like empathy, it *is* measurable. There are instruments that can measure empathy, but there is an experiment involved—not something that happens in a lab, but the research team is manipulating the environment, or manipulating some variable, and controlling everything else. So when you measure your outcome, in this case it would be your empathy levels and the person's experience in the museum that resulted in the change. That's very difficult to do in a museum setting. You have to control what people see, when they see it, how long they see it, and the order in which they see the installations within the exhibition. You have to match people on several things, such as age. You have to test their empathy levels before they enter the museum. It made more sense to pull back and ask exploratory questions and then see if there were underlying constructs that related to empathy, but that were not empathy in and of themselves.[7]

In other words, while empathy was integral to our objective for the exhibition, the evaluation needed to be grounded more in quantifiable metrics based on the nature of how and who we would sample. In the end, our solution was to broaden the query and attempt to measure sensory sensitivity: the level of stimulation and intensity individuals felt. Given the unprecedented nature of evaluating a groundbreaking exhibition, Verdín stressed that the investigation needed to start with questions to describe phenomena, a common approach in contexts where little empirical research exists on a given topic. Measuring sensory sensitivity as a multidimensional indicator of a visitor's response to the exhibition allowed us to tap into visitors' perceptual attunement, which is a more distal response than either situational or dispositional empathy.

THE EVOLUTION OF *SPEECHLESS*

Pioneering, experimental, exploratory, collaborative, accessible, inventive, multisensory, participatory, unconventional, innovative—these are all words that have been used to describe *speechless*. The exhibition explored the broad spectrum of sensory experiences and novel approaches to accessibility and modes of communication in the museum setting. It debuted six original, site-specific, participatory installations created by acclaimed and emerging artists and designers—Ini Archibong, Matt Checkowski, Misha Kahn, Steven and William Ladd, Laurie Haycock Makela, and Yuri Suzuki. The artists' immersive works invited museum visitors to touch sound, hear place, picture thought, and shape space.

"I entered into Sarah's vision because I felt an intuitive understanding of her interest in alternate communications, especially those emphasizing empathy," said Makela, who participated as an artist designing the show's catalog. "*speechless* was an opportunity to create something new."

To help the artists conceptualize work in response to the themes of the exhibition, we invited them to Dallas in September 2018 to join a group of scientists who challenged assumptions on disability, offered diverse perspectives, and encouraged the artists to explore fresh territory. This convening, as it became known, profoundly influenced the artists-designers and scientists—two groups that are not typically in dialogue with each other—who spent two days engaged in conversation, information exchange, and brainstorming alongside museum staff. By design, the conversation was wide-ranging and often unstructured, with a focus on issues of sensory processing, accessibility for people with differences, the relationship between the museum and the public, and the power of art to foster connection.

The convening was unusual on several fronts. For one thing, it brought together the artists-designers in advance of the opening of the exhibition, which rarely happens in group museum shows. As the designers noted, group shows can often feel like a competition to stand out from the pack. In contrast, *speechless* prompted them to work together to help chart the territory of the exhibition, fostering a spirit of inclusivity and collaboration.

It was also an unusual experience for the scientists and researchers who participated, which included Tandra Allen, Daniel Krawczyk, and Audette Rackley from the Center for BrainHealth; Jenny McGlothlin and Linda Thibodeaux from the Callier Center for Communication Disorders; Tina Fletcher from the Texas Woman's University; Bonnie Pitman, Distinguished Scholar in Residence at The University of Texas at Dallas; and Marianna Adams of Audience Focus Inc.[8] In a sentiment echoed by several others, Krawcyzk noted, "I felt like we covered a lot of innovative ideas that rarely get voiced because artists and scientists do not often talk."

The scientists and researchers' ideas offered insight not just for the artists' projects within the exhibition, but for their practices in general—and even for some personal discoveries about themselves. For example, Thibodeaux from the Callier Center presented on the effects of hearing loss across sensory systems, describing her work as grounded "more in wireless technology so cognitive resources can be freed up to make meaning rather than focus on the acoustic wave form—what did I just hear?" During the discussion, she described the auditory illusion known as the McGurk Effect: how perceivers of speech sounds blend information from their visual and auditory senses, effectively merging how one hears and sees a sound to create an entirely new one. For artist Suzuki, this was revelatory: "It was super relevant, incredible, especially . . . talking about the difference between visual perception of pronouncing a given word but without sound [the McGurk effect]." Another artist, hearing Thibodeaux's colleague McGlothlin discuss how children with sensory and development issues have difficulty regulating their own bodies, began to see similar patterns in himself. "The convening was awesome," he reported. "For selfish reasons I was heavily focused on [McGlothlin] because for the first time she accurately described my food weirdness to a T. And I never realized that there was more to it than just being weird about food. That was really interesting, eye-opening."[9] The environment was intimate and encouraged intense, thought-provoking discussions that ranged from the theoretical, scientific, and practical to the creative and deeply personal.

"It has been a life-impacting experience to connect with both artists and scientists for a common mission—to bridge the gap of communication," said Allen of the Center for BrainHealth. "Even though we are coming from divergent backgrounds and perspectives, we all agree that our human potential is unlimited, and understand there's not one direct path in life. Interacting with the artists and seeing their unique interpretation . . . has inspired my own creativity to think outside of what is typical."

Adams, a renowned evaluator and interpretive planning professional, attended the convening and distilled it into eight key findings/themes: clear messaging, design for visitor success, design for inclusivity, design for differences, design for personal connection, design for innovation, design for reflection and orientation, and the importance of ongoing process testing. These became guideposts for the project in general and for Verdín's methodology in developing the evaluation strategies.[10]

VISUALIZING THE INSTALLATION

In keeping with its spirit of experimentation and commitment to communicating in multiple ways, *speechless* explored alternative methods of conveying information about the exhibition to the visiting public. For example, we minimized written words and replaced them with aural, visual, and tactile cues to prioritize nonverbal learners and be as holistically accessible as possible.[11]

Entering the exhibition, after passing the soft, tactile title treatment at the entrance, visitors immediately encountered a wall with noise-canceling headphones and spiral-bound booklets for the visually impaired, both of which were freely available. The headphones provided a way to block noise for those who desired or required reduced auditory stimulation. (Additional noise-canceling headphones were provided in two of the artist's spaces.) The booklet included Braille versions of the exhibition's welcoming entrance text, descriptions of each work, bios of the artists, raised line drawings of the layout of the galleries, images of the artists, and the informational graphics for each space. In providing these resources to all, the goal was to destigmatize their use as a signifier of difference.

The central space featured a comfortable gathering area with several stools (see figure 6.1). The aim was to create a welcoming space that served as an information hub, communal gathering location, and physical palate cleanser between each installation experience. Visitors always passed back into this space before entering any other room. To orient them, six monitors with informational videos played on a continuous loop. The thirty-second videos featured each artist-designer in their installation space demonstrating how to interact with their work. The intention was for the videos to serve not only as an alternative to text instructions but also as a preview of sorts, allowing visitors to become familiar with each of the spaces in advance. The monitors floated above tactile color fields made from wheatpasted tissue paper, each of which was a different color to distinguish the artists. We decided to use color to delineate each space to avoid any sense of hierarchy that would be implied by using numbers or letters. We reviewed these color selections to ensure they had enough tonal distinction to accommodate for color vision deficiency.

The exploratoria, as we often referred to it, consisted of six individual spaces that emerged from the central hub like the arms of an octopus (see figure 6.2). The artists-designers tasked with exploring the exhibition's themes produced diverse and multifaceted works. The installations were interactive, immersive, provocative, and engaging.

Sarah Schleuning

Figure 6.1. *speechless*'s central space with introductory wall text, stools, intro videos for each installation, and wayfinding color bands. *Image courtesy Dallas Museum of Art*

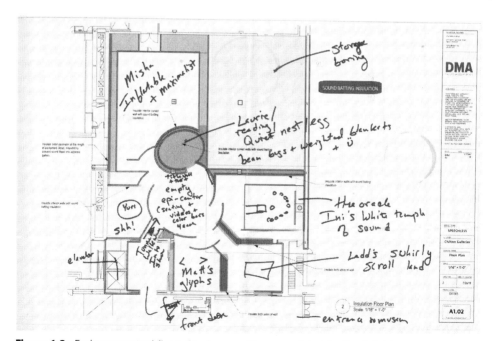

Figure 6.2. Early conceptual floor plan for *speechless*, annotated by Sarah Schleuning. *Image courtesy Dallas Museum of Art*

Figure 6.3. *theoracle*, 2019 Ini Archibong. Blown glass, brass, and water. Dallas Museum of Art. Commissioned by Dallas Museum of Art and High Museum of Art for the exhibition Speechless: Different by Design, 2019–2020. Purchased by Dallas Museum of Art, 2020.28.1.1. Image courtesy Dallas Museum of Art.
Image courtesy Dallas Museum of Art

   theoracle by Ini Archibong explored nontraditional and participatory ways of experiencing sound (see figure 6.3). Handblown glass capsules on brass stands encircled a larger glass obelisk and a pool of water. When visitors rotated the glass forms, they changed colors as they created various harmonious tones that emanated from the custom-built synthesizer behind the back wall. Archibong wanted visitors to create pure sound while employing the principles of cymatics; certain frequencies affected the motion of the water in the pool, thus illustrating sound through movement, shape, light, and color.[12]

   Glyph by Matt Checkowski consisted of a series of short, intimate films of each of the exhibition's artists-designers in dialogue (see figure 6.4). As the images played, a translation method Checkowski devised for this project turned the artists' words into images, using real-time internet search results. The work explored how interpretation varies based on both the creator and the receiver and whether a more visual mode of communication might provide for a different type of understanding than speech.[13]

   (T3)(8)*(J~)*([..")*(7ˆ)*(4=)* (F])*(Ilii.)*(A)*(!s)*(11)*('.v:')* by Misha Kahn is a winding garden composed of vibrant, dynamic inflatables that move in multiple ways, inflating and deflating continuously (see figure 6.5). Visitors could touch, sit, squeeze, and otherwise interact with the inflatable forms, observing the installation change around them and participating in the alteration.

Figure 6.4. *Glyph*, 2019. Matt Checkowski. Two channel video, color, sound. One-channel custom generative software, color, silent Media player, computer, internet connection, projectors. Dallas Museum of Art. Commissioned by Dallas Museum of Art and High Museum of Art for the exhibition Speechless: Different by Design, 2019–2020. Purchased by Dallas Museum of Art., 2020.28.4. *Image courtesy Dallas Museum of Art*

Figure 6.5. Schleuning and her children walking through Kahn's installation. *Image courtesy Dallas Museum of Art*

Figure 6.6. Visitors engaging with *Sound of the Earth* Chapter 2, 2019. Yuri Suzuki. Powder coated steel. Dallas Museum of Art. Commissioned by Dallas Museum of Art and High Museum of Art for the exhibition Speechless: Different by Design, 2019–2020, 2020.28.3. Purchased by Dallas Museum of Art. *Image courtesy Dallas Museum of Art*

Sound of the Earth Chapter 2 by Yuri Suzuki integrated audio crowdsourced from around the world (see figure 6.6). The work took the form of a dark, spherical sculpture with which visitors could interact by placing their ears against the surface. Each spot on the sphere represented a different area of the world and "whispered" back a corresponding sound sourced from that region, enabling visitors to experience the globe in a fresh way, beyond text and words. Anyone around the world could submit audio via the DMA's website.[14]

Scroll Space by Steven and William Ladd was a vibrant and tactile installation that included a room created entirely of tens of thousands of hand-rolled textile "scrolls" (see figure 6.7). These scrolls were made in collaboration with seventeen hundred community members in Dallas and Atlanta through the Ladd brothers' community engagement program Scrollathon®, which brings the arts to underserved populations through hands-on creative workshops. The gallery also included a mural composed of portraits of all the participants who created the scrolls.[15]

Laurie Haycock Makela created the graphic identity for the exhibition and designed both of its publications (see figure 6.8). In Makela's space, her exhibition catalog design in proof-page form lined the acoustic-foam-paneled walls. This space doubled as a place of reflection and deescalation, inviting people to sit and rest in comfortable rocking chairs and utilize weighted lap blankets and/or noise-canceling headphones, all of which are means to self-soothe.

Sarah Schleuning

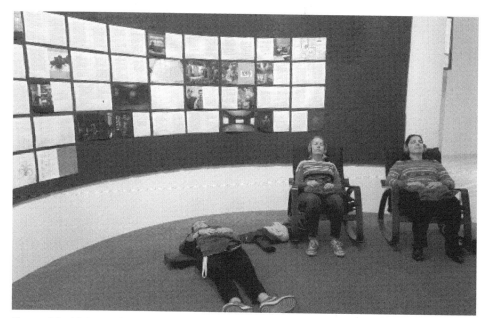

Figure 6.7. Interior of the structure with walls made of the scrolls looking into gallery with photo wall of participants.

Dallas wall commissioned for Scroll Space, 2019. Steven Ladd, William Ladd. Wood, textiles, pins, rubber bands, and glue. Dallas Museum of Art. Commissioned by Dallas Museum of Art and High Museum of Art for the exhibition Speechless: Different by Design, 2019-2020. Purchased by Dallas Museum of Art., 2020.28.2.

Image courtesy Dallas Museum of Art

Figure 6.8. Visitors relaxing in Makela's space using various de-escalating tools including noise-canceling headphones, rockers, and weighted lap pads. *Image courtesy Dallas Museum of Art*

"From its inception, the project piqued my interests and seemed suited to my design experience," Makela said. "However, it came at a time when thought I was no longer able to access those abilities due to a traumatic brain injury. Literally, I thought the project was over my head. Sarah trusted me to use that fear and neurological difference to enrich and develop the design for *speechless.*"[16]

The only written text present in each installation space was the name and image of the artist(s) and the title and date of the work. Rather than more descriptive labels, we offered simplified drawings of charming anthropomorphic blobs offering ways to interact and engage with the individual works. They were designed to encourage rather than chastise, offering a positive way to interact with the works, if the visitor desired. They were also present in the Braille publication available upon entry.

As with anything experimental, the responses to these materials were mixed, according to our formal evaluation, as well as anecdotal evidence and observation. While some reported a desire for more text and more explanation about the installations, many visitors felt engaged and even empowered by the process of discovery. They also expressed appreciation that the experience encouraged a sense of wonder not mediated by text-based interpretations. As with the individual projects and the spirit of the installation, the graphics and interpretive and experiential elements were designed with the intention to decenter our standard practice that favors text-based learning while still following universal design for learning best practices.

UNPACKING THE VISITOR RESEARCH STUDY

"[*speechless*] was a breath of fresh air for my brain," said a museum visitor, one of the 235 people who took part in a survey about the exhibition for the larger visitor research study conducted by Verdín.[17] The rigorous academic study, which was approved by an external institutional review board, had two phases. Phase 1 was the survey, conducted February 1–16, 2020, which queried adult museum visitors with seventeen questions immediately after they viewed *speechless*. We wanted to learn how they felt and what they wondered. Phase 2, a follow-up telephone interview conducted February 18–March 13, 2020, engaged eight of those respondents in a longer dialogue.

The design of the Phase 1 survey instrument was informed by conversations between myself and Verdín, as well as a walk-through of the installations while under construction in late 2019. Guided by antiableism and an expansive view of neurodiversity beyond clinical definitions, Verdín researched existing scientific literature to explore how indicators of human sensory phenomena, including individual sensitivities, thresholds, and preferences, could be measured reliably. The underlying logic was that if the artists' intentions were to facilitate opportunities for visitors to interact with art through touch, sound, sight, vestibular, and proprioceptive input, then the survey should capture those

Sarah Schleuning

Figure 6.9. Information graphics for the installation. *Image courtesy Dallas Museum of Art*

varied responses. While exploring these valid measures of sensory-related responses, though, another goal soon emerged. Much of the prior scientific literature about museum experiential learning indicated that shifts in thinking and feeling are facilitated through socially mediated interactions. As a result, Verdín proposed expanding the research beyond descriptive aims to include questions that could answer whether and how social experiences were influenced by differences in sensory sensitivities.

The whole evaluation component was based around four research questions:

1. What is the relationship between visitors' sensory-sensitivity responses and their level of emotional stimulation in each room and in the exhibition as a whole?
2. Is this relationship mediated by visitors' association with a person with a neurological difference?
3. Are visitors' perceptions of the exhibition as a social experience predicted by visitors' sensory-sensitivity responses, emotional intensity, and association with a person with a neurological difference or special need?
4. How do visitors describe their lived experiences of speechless: different by design?

When visitors exited the exhibition, they were met by a research assistant who had been trained by Verdín in survey administration. Visitors were told that participation in the survey was voluntary and that they would receive a DMA postcard as a small honorarium upon completion of the survey. Visitors who agreed to take the survey were given an iPad that displayed the opening text of the Qualtrics survey, beginning with an informed consent form, followed by the survey items.

To answer the first three research questions, Verdín downloaded the raw data from this survey on Qualtrics and used SPSS, a commercially available statistical software, to run a series of descriptive and inferential analyses. (Detailed statistical results are documented in her final evaluation report [VRS].[18]) To answer the first question—What is the relationship between visitors' sensory-sensitivity responses and their level of emotional stimulation in each room and in the exhibition as a whole?—she performed a series of Pearson correlational analyses. She did not find statistically significant correlations between visitors' sensitivity and emotional stimulation in the exhibition as a whole nor in the individual artists' installations—with one exception. When visitors reported lower levels of sensory sensitivity in theoracle, they experienced high levels of emotional stimulation. Qualitative data from the follow-up phone interviews may shed light on this surprising finding. First, this room differed from others in that gallery attendants were asked to provide instructions for interacting with the art, suggesting that their presence and guidance may have had an emotionally comforting effect on some visitors. Second, participants with neurodivergent children reported that the combination of sensory stimuli facilitated their children's ability to interact more autonomously than in traditional art spaces, leading to a more positive emotional response from the parent.

Because the exhibition as a whole did not reveal a statistically significant association between sensitivity and emotional stimulation, Verdín could not conduct a mediation model to answer the second question: Is this relationship mediated by visitors' association with a person with a neurological difference? However, she did conduct a correlational analysis between sensory sensitivity and visitors who identified as having a neurological difference or being the caregiver of a person who did. We wanted to investigate whether sensory sensitivity was greater for visitors who were neurodivergent themselves or in close relationship to someone who is. This hypothesis was supported by the data, which showed a weak but significant correlation ($r = .116$, $p < .05$) between these two variables.

To answer the third research question—Are visitors' perceptions of the exhibition as a social experience predicted by visitors' sensory-sensitivity responses, emotional intensity, and association with a person with a neurological difference or special need?—Verdín conducted a multiple regression analysis and found a small but statistically significant effect size indicating that a visitor's combined experience of sensory sensitivity, emotional intensity, and association with a neurodiverse person predicted almost 20 percent of their social experience score ($R^2 = .19$, $p < .001$).

Finally, to answer the fourth research question—How do visitors describe their lived experiences of *speechless: different by design*?—Verdín conducted phone interviews with eight participants who agreed to be contacted after completion of the survey. She used a semistructured interview guide to delve more deeply into the nuances of visitors' sensory, emotional, and social experiences while interacting with the exhibition. She conducted the interviews either in person or on a cell phone and recorded them using the Tape-a-Call app. She uploaded the interview audio files to NVivo, a commercially available qualitative software program, and coded them using thematic analytic strategies. The qualitative analyses yielded four themes: (1) stretching your mind, (2) seeing through others, (3) scaffolded learning, and (4) original and inspiring. These results, along with a content analysis of the open-ended questions answered by the 235 visitors who completed the digital survey, are described in more detail below.

In keeping with the exhibition, the digital survey was designed to have a strong nonverbal component, using images and emojis to connote place and emotion (see figure 6.10). It opened with three open-ended questions. One of them asked visitors to describe their reaction to *speechless*. In the responses, some of the words that came up repeatedly included: inspired, happy, intrigued, calm, relaxed, and creative. Eighty-two percent of responses were explicitly positive, while 18 percent were neutral or negative. Some of the most common

After experiencing *speechless*, I felt (fill in the blank):

_____

Move the slider to rate your level of EMOTIONAL INTENSITY (i.e., from sleepy/relaxed to over-stimulated) experienced in this room.

Move the slider to rate your level of EMOTIONAL INTENSITY (i.e., from sleepy/relaxed to over-stimulated) experienced in this room.

Move the slider to rate your level of EMOTIONAL INTENSITY (i.e., from sleepy/relaxed to over-stimulated) experienced in this room.

Figure 6.10. Example of Survey for *speechless*. *Image courtesy Dallas Museum of Art*

ambiguous words visitors used to describe their experience were *overwhelmed, anxious, disturbed*, and *confused*.

In the *different by design* interview with Verdín and myself, where we discuss the VSR entitled "There is No Such Thing as an Average Visitor," Verdín explains:

> It wasn't that those eighteen percent were primarily negative, it was that some of those comments were ambiguous. I see that as a positive on multiple levels, one because eighty-two percent positive is a good number, and two because that balance of the eighteen percent is not explicitly negative. Anytime we are trying to buck the status quo, there needs to be a margin for that sort of disorientation or disequilibrium that ultimately is going to produce change.[19]

That discrepancy is one of the through-themes of the exhibition: everyone is different. The study, among other things, sought to discover how these differences manifested in terms of people's responses to the works on view. While the analysis is reflective of significant associations between sensory sensitivity and emotional intensity of individual installations, the implication is that aesthetic experiences like those found in *speechless* offer surprising experiences of empowerment for those seeking sensory input that may not be met within the confines of a more traditional art museum.

Figure 6.11. Visitor responses to survey questions as reimaged by Laurie Haycock Makela (pp. 94–95). *Image courtesy Dallas Museum of Art*

BOX 6.1. OTHER KEY STATISTICAL FINDINGS FROM THE VRS

- Twenty-nine percent of survey participants had an association with (dis)ability or neurodiversity—either themselves or close relatives or both.
- Eighty percent of visitors with a child with a special need or difference had a positive response to the exhibition.
- Seventy-three percent of visitors who self-reported as having a special need or difference or health concern had a positive response to the exhibition.
- Eighty-six percent of visitors with no association to neurodiversity or difference had a positive response to the exhibition.[1]

Note

1. Schleuning and Gollin, *different by design: the speechless report*, 86.

Part of the transparency of this project was for all contributors to reflect with candor on the challenges they faced. For Verdín's part, she eloquently expressed how her role and previous knowledge about the DMA's visitors affected her approach:

As the person designing the evaluation, the biggest challenge was not knowing how different the group of people that would eventually attend *speechless* might be from the general visitor population of the museum. I was familiar with a profile of the general visitor based on the investigation I led for the DMA in 2018-19 that analyzed the museum's audience, so I had to base a lot of my assumptions out of my knowledge of the general visitorship.

But of course, I knew that this group of visitors would probably be and look different, from a data perspective. That made me a little uneasy, because as we were in conversation about what questions to ask and how to ask them and how to scale them and whether to do it pictorially or with words or a combination of the two, I would ask myself whether it was appropriate for the population of visitors that would come to the show? And of course, I didn't know the answer; none of us did.

Knowing this made the second phase of the evaluation key. The follow-up phone survey was part of her calibration to offer nuance and exploration into the individuality of our visitors and the experience they had. As she herself concluded, "A good evaluation data collection tool is going to be calibrated so it's tapping into some of the nuances that reflect differences in the visitor body. However, when we added the interview component, we allowed for

Sarah Schleuning

people to give us more of their rich descriptions of their lived experience and interactions, which helped to fill out those missing edges."[20] For example, one visitor she spoke to, who has attention-deficit/hyperactivity disorder (ADHD) and is the parent of two neurodivergent daughters, described having a higher tolerance for sensory stimulation when she tries imagining the world from her children's perspective. This was the case in Checkowski's installation, where she herself struggled with the amount of sensory input but acknowledged that her daughters enjoyed the intense stimulation, underscoring the importance of tolerating differences.

LESSONS LEARNED

Our evaluation findings expanded our understanding of the importance of effectively reaching a wider audience. Viewed collectively, the work of this project is simply an iterative step in a much longer journey. The following is a preliminary list of next steps for museums to consider exploring to cultivate innovation around accessibility. The ideas range from very specific and particular to the experience of the DMA to much broader and/or more holistic for the museum field in general.[21]

- **deescalation spaces:** To continue to advocate for spaces that offer opportunities for individuals to decompress, center themselves, and self-soothe.
- **flexible spaces:** The central space in *speechless* was the type of flexible gathering area that could be replicated in other exhibitions, or even in spaces in the museum that are not within galleries.
- **noise-canceling headphones**: Neurodivergent visitors and their caregivers may more comfortably experience the art when offered aids like noise-canceling headphones throughout galleries, a more friendly and accessible approach than only having them available by special request at the visitor service desk.
- **staff training and education:** For an accessibility-related initiative to succeed, all staff involved need to be well-informed and trained on best practices. It is important to create strong pathways of communication throughout the institution, implement ways to monitor whether staff members may be struggling with the information you communicate, and invest in more in-depth training for all staff members, both paid and volunteer, who interact regularly with visitors.

For *speechless*, I and other team members provided training sessions in the lead-up to the exhibition focusing on content, security, and the visitor experience. In hindsight, we should have continued conducting these sessions throughout the run of the show, to give staff the chance to share issues or questions that came up once it was open, and collectively explore solutions.

There is also a need to build flexibility into a museum's procedures so that when projects like *speechless*, which diverge from the traditional ways of operating, require additional trainings and dialogue, there is a strong commitment to the process throughout the run of the exhibition by means of listening, evaluation, and dialogue within the institution and community before, during, and after the experience.

- **Nontext-based interpretation**: For this project, we provided information graphics and videos throughout the galleries in lieu of text-based labels and interpretation. As we expected, visitors said this made a difference in their experience of the exhibition. One participant in the study found the lack of written interpretation freeing, noting that not having to read text panels gave her a sense of relief from the self-imposed expectation that she must consume textual information as a normative behavioral practice in an art museum. Experimenting with these nontext-based approaches, either in tandem with or without text, will provide for audience members who don't always prioritize written language as their primary means of gathering information about art. Alternative interpretation approaches could also explore other sensory options, such as sound, taste, or smell. Likewise, museums could explore digital options to provide information, context, and interpretation, such as podcasts, videos, and graphics.
- **Interpretation for the visually impaired and others:** Booklets offering information in Braille and with raised images were available for everyone, with the objective of making the show more accessible for the visually impaired. They were utilized and enjoyed by many visitors, not only the visually impaired, and observation suggests that they helped increase awareness of, interest in, and empathy for sensory differences. Similarly, small but meaningful actions include welcoming the hearing-impaired through measures like captioning videos.

  Another tool the DMA regularly provides is communication cards, which use labeled pictures to help people express common needs or feelings. While these cards were originally developed for visitors on the autism spectrum, they have also proven very helpful to those who are learning or do not speak English. Communication cards typically use a system of symbols called the Picture Exchange Communication System (PECS), but this system can have frustrating limitations in nuance, emotions, and aesthetics. (In fact, this frustration was an aspect of the original impetus for *speechless*.) As an alternative, our museum might explore developing card communication resources using works of art in the collection.
- **Providing experiences for our wide range of visitors:** *speechless* was multisensory and multimodal, providing avenues of engagement for many different learning strengths and styles. This emphasis on inclusion and

neurodiversity can be further explored at the DMA and elsewhere in exhibitions and programming.

- **Iterations and evaluations:** Providing opportunities and funding sources, even on a small scale, to be more flexible, iterative, and reflective is critical to forward motion. Having a dedicated source of funding for opportunities and capacity to do this, both while projects are still up and after they conclude, provides ways for the institution to continue to grow and build upon opportunities explored. In our case, the planning work for the evaluation and follow-up publication for the project has been invaluable.
- **Think tank:** All the recommendations would be predicated on an ongoing commitment to discussion and exploration and would benefit from the establishment of a think tank or brainstorming group dedicated to creativity, innovation, and even rocking the boat.

NEXT STEPS: RECOMMENDATIONS FOR THE FUTURE

Beyond sharing and unpacking the VRS's findings, *different by design* offered a space to reflect on this pioneering project and suggest ideas, and even concrete recommendations, for museums beyond the DMA. How could we capitalize on this project to make valuable contributions to museum practice? Developing *speechless* confirmed what we already suspected: that the museum visitor is not monolithic, and that the neurodivergent population is not typically a primary consideration for museums. We know it is time to address this omission. The question we are left with is: How might we advocate for and expand our understanding of difference and disability while offering more accessible spaces and experiences?

NOTES

1. I am deeply grateful for the support that made all elements of this project possible. Above all, I appreciate the willingness of the Dallas Museum of Art, the High Museum of Art, and the artists-designers to invest a great deal of time and resources to enter this creative experiment with me. We did not always know where we were going, and I believe the journey was all the richer thanks to our willingness to explore.
2. Due to the COVID-19 pandemic, the show closed one week early at the DMA and never traveled to the High. All data of the project and Visitor Research Study are from the DMA.
3. The 2020 publication was copublished by the Dallas Museum of Art and the High Museum of Art and distributed by Yale University Press.
4. My deep gratitude to Dr. Verdín, who worked extensively with me and the rest of the team. She has been invaluable in this essay as well, offering feedback and shaping the content to be more focused towards the field of evaluation.

5. Both publications were the product of numerous individuals. Special appreciation to coeditor on the 2020 publication, *speechless: different by design*, Andrea Gollin, Laurie Haycock Makela, and Eric Zeidler. The same individual came together for the *different by design* report with Andrea Gollin coauthored with me as well. All these individuals along with Azucena Verdín worked tirelessly on this passion project to finesse and fine-turn the words and visuals presented in the publication. This chapter stands on the shoulders of their great work as well as countless others who reviewed, discussed, and challenged our thinking to make this the best work possible.

6. Please see appendix E in *different by design: the speechless project* at speechless.dme.org for a more complete listing. The AAM blog posting are 1 January 2020's "Speechless: A sensory exhibition charts a new path to accessibility in learning" (https://www.aam-us.org/2020/01/01/speechless-a-sensory-exhibition-charts-a-new-path-to-accessibility-in-learning/) and 20 January 2023's "Different by Design: A New, Inclusive Framework for Accessible Museum Exhibitions" (https://www.aam-us.org/2023/01/20/different-by-design-a-new-inclusive-framework-for-accessible-museum-exhibitions/).

7. Schleuning and Gollin, *different by design: the speechless report*, 63.

8. Additional biographical information for the scientists and researchers can be found in appendix H (pp. 166–69) of *different by design: the speechless report*. Likewise, biographical information for the artists-designers is included in the "Installations" section of the same publication.

9. These findings can be explored further in Marianna Adams's "notes and reflections on the convening" published in *different by design; the speechless project*, 158–65 and Sarah Schleuning's "opening a dialogue: the convening" published in *speechless: different by design*, 16–23.

10. Both Adams's original assessment (161–62) and Verdín's reference (124) to it can be found in *different by design: the speechless report*.

11. This work was done in consultation with the scientists and researchers who participated in the Convening, notably Tina Fletcher, whose expertise includes a focus on improving participation in the arts for visitors with special needs. Members of the museum team who had key roles in this process included Kerry Butcher, former manager of the Center for Creative Connections; Jaclyn Le, former senior graphic designer; Skye Malish-Olson, former exhibition designer; Emily Schiller, head of interpretation; and Emily Wiskera, former manager of access programs, current interpretation specialist.

12. A subsequent iteration of *theoracle* was presented at the DMA exhibition *To Be Determined*, for which Archibong reconceptualized the installation in part to address how COVID-19 protocols silenced this work, which had previously been activated by human touch. Against the backdrop of the social unrest of the Black Lives Matter movement, Archibong also reflected on the realities of growing up as a black male in America. Consequently, he altered the harmonic tones from the serene beauty in *speechless* to an imposing drone, and the once-inviting, glowing sculptures were dimmed and rendered untouchable. The work was renamed *theoracle*. Both works are part of the DMA's collection.

13. The work is now part of the DMA's collection.

14. The piece was acquired by the DMA, and a new and digital iteration of it was formulated during the pandemic. Titled *Sound of the Earth the Pandemic Chapter*, as of this writing it continues to gather sounds from around the world, engendering a sense of community by providing access to these sounds through the online platform (access it at https://globalsound. dma.org/).

15. Portions of *Scroll Space* were acquired by the Dallas Museum of Art; the High Museum also acquired parts of the installation with each institution collecting aspects of the piece that featured scrolls from their respective communities.

16. Schleuning and Gollin, *different by design: the speechless report*, 113.

17. All elements listed can be found in *different by design: the speechless report*. The full study is reproduced in appendix A of *different by design*. The survey questions are the subject of appendix B, and the phone interview questions are in appendix C. Additionally, the study is discussed in depth in "There is No Such Thing as an Average Visitor," the conversation between Schleuning and Verdín in this publication.

18. The full report was published as appendix A in *different by design: the speechless report*, p. 122–39. The analysis of the survey relied on both Verdín's VRS and her input and revisions to this essay. I am grateful for the time she invested to make sure we accurately reflected her findings.

19. Schleuning and Gollin, *different by design: the speechless report*, 56.

20. Schleuning and Gollin, *different by design: the speechless report*, 60.

21. These have been published both in the AAM blog and in *different by design*.

BIBLIOGRAPHY

PBS NewsHour "The 'speechless: different by design' Exhibit Uses Brain Science to Inform Art." February 18, 2020.

Samaha, Barry. "How The Dallas Museum of Art's New Exhibition Is Broadening The Idea Of Visual Communication." *Forbes*, November 11, 2019.

Schleuning, Sarah. *speechless: different by design*. Dallas: DMA and HMA, 2019.

Schleuning, Sarah, and Andrea Gollin. *different by design: the speechless report*. files.dma. org/speechless/speechless_epub.pdf, 2021.

Singer, Dan. "Please Touch the Art." Dallas Morning News Online November 8, 2019; in print November 10, 2019.

7

Beyond Participant Data

ALTERNATIVE WAYS OF MEASURING IMPACT

Karen Breece, Kelsey Van Voorst, and Maia Swinson

A Memory Café is a program designed to encourage socialization and memory reconnaissance for people experiencing the symptoms of dementia. Following an open-ended format, the program invites these people and their caregivers to mingle and join in activities led by a trained facilitator, which can include everything from crafts to animal handling to board games.

At the Memory Café in the anecdote above, participants visited a barn at Conner Prairie, where guests can interact with farm animals like goats, sheep, rabbits, and young chicks. As this reflection from the program's facilitator describes, the animals functioned as a social object that connected the participants to their own childhoods.[1] This is what we mean by memory reconnaissance: involving all five senses in programming to help trigger participants' memories. There is some evidence to suggest that while Alzheimer's attacks more recently formed memories, it can leave older ones from someone's childhood and early adulthood relatively intact.[2] Our goal with the memory reconnaissance framework is to use Conner Prairie's collections (both living and nonliving) to help people with dementia reconnect with those memories and their caregivers at the same time.

Conner Prairie is a uniquely designed museum in a northern suburb of Indianapolis, Indiana. We were originally founded as a historic site and living history museum, but our focus has grown to encompass historic trades like carpentry, weaving, and ceramics; historic agriculture; playspaces for children of all ages; and holiday festivals. Our collection not only includes objects but also livestock and our staff of expert educators, costumed interpreters, and tradesmen. When we were thinking about expanding our program offerings to the aging population of our surrounding communities, we discovered Memory Cafés as a format that could make use of all these aspects of our site and organization.

While there are other models of facilitated museum programs for people with dementia, including structured tours like the MeetMe at MOMA format,[3] we decided to look to another popular model that originated outside of the field. Psychologist Dr. Bère Miesen launched the first Memory Café in a lecture room at Leiden University in the Netherlands in 1997, and the format then spread to numerous nursing homes, restaurants, and community centers in Europe and the United States.[4] National organizations like Dementia Friends and local ones like the Central Indiana Center on Aging (CICOA) started experimenting with programs like these because their informal structure appealed more than tightly controlled formats to individuals and caregivers who desired freedom and independent living. For these reasons, Conner Prairie decided to adopt the Memory Café model, whose flexibility we found to serve us and our guests the best. Through reflection and iterative development, we were able to create a program that was effective, impactful, and sustainable.

You'll notice that we did not mention data collection. In fact, other than some basic early feedback instruments, we have intentionally not collected data from our participants. So, what are we doing in a book all about evaluating accessibility programs in museums? In this chapter, we offer a unique, and perhaps controversial, perspective: that not every program needs you to collect data to demonstrate that it is effective for participants. Especially if in the process of collecting data, there is a possibility of causing an already vulnerable and marginalized population more harm. While we do believe it important to use data to inform decision making, we maintain there are times it is better to look at other sources for this data. For our Memory Cafés, for instance, we have relied on case studies from other museums and medical studies that confirmed the effectiveness of the program's elements. Because of the vulnerability of the population we are serving, we felt this was a more ethically sound way forward than collecting new data from program participants. Ultimately, we decided to rely on secondary evaluation data and research to shape our program and understand our findings, but we encourage you to read through our decision-making process and come to your own conclusion.

In the following pages, we will examine different research considerations when working with people with dementia, including the preexistence of secondary research and other evaluation studies, how ongoing reflection and benchmarking has shaped the development of our program during the first four years of its existence, and the successes that keep encouraging Conner Prairie to pursue accessibility programming.

Karen Breece, Kelsey Van Voorst, and Maia Swinson

INITIAL DEVELOPMENT OF THE PROGRAM

In late 2017, leadership at CICOA and Dementia Friends Indiana (the state chapter of global organization Dementia Friends) approached the executive leadership team at Conner Prairie about the opportunity they saw to provide engaging experiences at the museum for aging citizens experiencing signs of Alzheimer's and dementia. They believed Conner Prairie would be the perfect place for these types of programming, as using items and artifacts from the past can help trigger memories in older generations who may experience memory loss.

To begin the partnership, coaches from CICOA and Dementia Friends Indiana trained a handful of Conner Prairie staff in dementia-friendly practices. At the end of these sessions, the staff became "dementia champions" who could then train other staff in what they had learned. Through two-hour sessions offered every other month, more than thirty-five staff members across multiple departments in the museum had completed training by early 2019.

The training sessions started with information about what Alzheimer's disease is, how it physically affects the brain, and the side effects, like dementia, that come along with it as it progresses. Then, staff learned how Alzheimer's symptoms manifest in people. As we learned, the most common symptom is memory loss, but the disease can also make people more easily irritable, slower to respond with answers to questions, forgetful of names of everyday objects (for example, calling a watch something like a "wrist clock"), and low in energy for social experiences. Alzheimer's can be a very isolating disease. So, creating experiences that promote socialization with others with the help of utilizing the five senses can be extremely effective to help the brain stay active as the disease progresses. Some of these best practices include patience when waiting for a response (dementia and Alzheimer's patients often need to take more time to put together a response to questions), speaking softly, and using simple, consistent language.

As this training worked its way through our ranks, we were ready to begin our Memory Café. The museum picked Kelsey Van Voorst, one of the authors of this chapter, to lead the program. She designed it to be a safe space where individuals with Alzheimer's and other forms of dementia could come without judgment to engage their five senses, initiate conversation, and potentially regain memories that have faded over time. We developed this approach using research best practices from both the medical and museum fields.

EFFECTIVE MEMORY CAFÉ PROGRAMMING

In the later half of 2017, Conner Prairie staff researched and trained up on what made programs like Memory Cafés successful for individuals living with dementia and/or Alzheimer's. What did we learn? For one thing, Dementia Friends and CICOA suggested that all programs should include intentional utilization of one or more of the five senses. Studies have shown that activities that engage your senses (especially sound, taste, and smell) are helpful in exercising the part of the brain that is responsible for short- and long-term memory.[5] Playing music from a person's past or cooking something that is reminiscent of a favorite food from childhood, for example, can help them find memories they may have forgotten. We have followed this advice in all of the Memory Cafés we have hosted at Conner Prairie.

Another component of an effective Memory Café we learned to consider is the physical accessibility of the program for participants. For example, there needs to be ample seating for folks to sit and rest, especially if part of your program involves movement. You should provide transportation for any extended distances or difficult terrain you expect participants to travel (we use golf carts and a tram to transport guests around our uneven gravel paths at Conner Prairie). And it is always helpful to have wheelchairs available just in case someone may need one during the program.

Finally, we learned the importance of creating a space where people feel welcome to come as they are without being judged, so they are more inclined to communicate. Alzheimer's and other forms of dementia can be very isolating, and communication can become a real struggle for some, as words that were once common vocabulary become harder to find, and ideas and feelings take longer to express. To overcome this isolation, people need to feel encouraged to communicate despite these difficulties. It may be hard to find a word for something that used to be common, or it may take a bit longer to express an idea or a feeling. That is why it is important to create a space where people feel welcome to come as they are and that they are not being judged in any way.

EARLY PROGRAMMING

In August of 2018, Conner Prairie held its very first Memory Café. We brought out some historic items in our collection and put them in the center of each table in the room where the program took place. Once all guests were seated, we encouraged them to pick up the items, investigate them closely, and then try to guess what they were. This activity is called object handling, which prompts different memories, emotions, and cognitive associations.[6] Interacting with these physical objects can help to trigger memories and emphasize connections to parts of the participants' identity like relationships, religion, nature, and society.[7] We then invite them to share these memories with others, if they choose.

Figure 7.1. Memory Café participants pet a chicken being handled by Conner Prairie staff.
Conner Prairie

Figure 7.2. A Memory Café participant pets a rabbit being handled by Conner Prairie staff.
Conner Prairie

Figure 7.3. A Conner Prairie staff member holds a goat while a Memory Café participant watches. *Conner Prairie*

Figure 7.4. A Memory Café participant looks at a rabbit being handled by Conner Prairie staff. *Conner Prairie*

There were some moments of beautiful conversation at that very first Memory Café. Participants had a wonderful time chatting with each other and investigating the items on the table. One woman who held an antique curry comb remembered that she and her sister had to go out every morning and brush the horses on her parents' farm. No one could figure out what the roach trap was, but it did start some great dialogue about pest control and tricks participants had learned to keep bugs out of their homes.

After the success of the first program, we realized that planning for future editions didn't need to be that time-consuming or cost prohibitive. Conner Prairie has so many resources at its disposal, between passionate staff, abundant green space, and rich historical context, that it was fairly easy and inexpensive to put together a successful Memory Café. Each café had an entirely different theme but was always intentionally designed to spark conversation with guests and engage their senses.

OPPORTUNITIES FOR CAREGIVERS

Memory Cafés are not only helpful for those living with dementia and Alzheimer's, but for their caregivers as well. To begin with, they give caregivers the rare opportunity to relax from the stress of caring for their loved ones and let the program facilitators be the caretakers for a while. They also allow them to socialize and receive support from other caregivers,[8] and to connect with their loved ones in a new way through the activities.[9] It can be such a gift for a caregiver to not have to worry about their loved one for an hour or two while they are actively engaging in a social activity with others in a similar situation.

As the Memory Café programs at Conner Prairie continued to grow, the museum started to see more and more return patrons to the program. We would usually get between twelve to sixteen people attending each program, two thirds of whom had attended Memory Cafés at Conner Prairie before. It became a reliable monthly resource for individuals living with dementia and Alzheimer's and their caregivers. Guests looked forward to socializing with each other every month and even began friendships outside of the Memory Café. Participants would recognize each other and catch up like old friends who haven't seen one another in a while.

INITIAL EVALUATION

When we began doing Memory Cafés, Conner Prairie did not have an internal evaluator, but we still were curious as to what impact the program had on the participants. So, we did some rudimentary pre- and postassessments of participants, measuring their mood before and after a pilot of the program using smiling, neutral, and frowning face images. Of the groups (participant and caregiver) that we surveyed, 100 percent noticed a positive change in their mood after the program concluded. We conducted another survey for a Memory Day program that we did in May of 2019 with similar results.

INCREASED PROGRAM ENGAGEMENT

Guests continued to come to the Memory Cafés, and staff continued to get trained. In May of 2019, Conner Prairie hosted Memory Day, which was a full day of activities and resources for individuals living with Alzheimer's and dementia and their caregivers. We had a musical performance from a seniors-only brass band, tactile art therapy, companion animals, and lectures from content experts about how Alzheimer's affects the brain and how music, art, and movement therapy can help alleviate the effects and symptoms. In our evaluation with participants, 100 percent said that they had a better mood and outlook after attending the event.

The Memory Café became a popular program with the Conner Prairie guests and members, and we continued to offer it monthly for the rest of 2019. For the most part, people attended independently with their caregivers, but on occasion we had assisted living communities and memory care facilities visit for a group outing. Attendance was a bit sporadic, but for more popular editions, we had about thirteen to sixteen participants, including caregivers. However, in March of 2020 the Memory Café program came to a screeching halt, along with many other public programs.

Later in this chapter, we will dive into how we pivoted the Memory Café program in response to the COVID-19 pandemic, and share some lessons learned from that experience. For now, we'll share that one benefit of the disruption was that, once we were ready to come out of our organizational lockdown period, we could look at the program with fresh eyes. We concluded that Memory Cafés still met an important need of the community, but that we needed to change some of the logistical operations and program delivery methods to truly meet the needs of the audience, and that the organization needed to be completely onboard and committed to make the programs successful.

RESEARCH CONSIDERATIONS

Planning and executing a program with participants' needs in mind is only part of the work. Another essential part is ensuring ongoing organizational support and agility, reflecting on the successes and failures of the program and making adjustments as needed. For neurotypical audiences, this usually involves collecting data—often through a survey, interview, focus group, or observation—on what participants think of the program and drawing conclusions from it as a part of an evaluation process. However, even though Conner Prairie did eventually hire an internal evaluator, we still decided not to do ongoing evaluation for Memory Cafés using the traditional methods listed above. Weighing the cost of and benefits of data collection for participants, the ability to gain consent from participants to participate in research, the lack of funder requirements for evaluation, and, importantly, the ability to rely on lessons learned from other institutions and programs through published evaluation reports and secondary research, we decided that the program was not appropriate for collecting audience data.

The next few pages will walk you through how we made these decisions and offer advice about how you can weigh each factor in your own studies, especially those that target people with cognitive disabilities like dementia. Although this is outside the scope of this chapter, we would suggest that you also consider consulting an institutional review board (IRB), a committee made up of people trained to oversee ethics in research studies, when making your own decision about whether to collect new data on your program. This would be especially important if you plan on your work ever leaving the confines of your museum. Here is what we considered.

COST AND BENEFIT

First and foremost, consider what the potential risks and benefits of data collection are for the population you would be collecting from. Risks may not be obvious, but they are present at every part of the research process. Think through the questions you may ask and how you will eventually store the data. Is there, at any point in the process, a chance that data could be leaked and someone may lose their right to privacy? Will the questions you ask potentially cause stress if someone is not able to answer them?

Weigh the vulnerability of your audience. Research guidelines often consider people with cognitive disabilities a vulnerable population, meaning that they are at greater risk of being exploited and may not have the capacity to give informed consent. Determining capacity may sound simple enough, but for people with dementia it can often be challenging.[10]

While not a risk, per se, we also advise you to consider how data collection can be a detriment to many visitors' museum experiences. Is there a way you can seamlessly fit data collection into the course of the program or museum visit without asking someone to exhaust themselves giving feedback? Consider not only what method of data collection you use, but even the length of the questions you ask.

Gauging benefits is much more straightforward. An incentive is one way study participants can directly benefit from research: will you pay people for their time, in either cash or a museum gift card? You should also consider how the study will benefit participants indirectly: Feedback can lead to the program improving, giving them and others a better experience. If it demonstrates that the program makes a difference, it can be used to garner more financial support and keep the program going.

In our case, we weighed the risks and benefits to participants and decided that the potential risks outweighed the benefits. We could see and hear what the program offered participants: a safe, welcoming, and accessible outing to a museum. We also knew from preexisting literature that these types of museum programs offer documented benefits to people with dementia and their caregivers. We decided we could use this preexisting literature to garner internal and external support for the program and form sustaining partnerships. There was little benefit to us reproducing this existing research at our museum, especially since the risks of data collection were higher because of the vulnerability of the population.

ABILITY TO GAIN INFORMED CONSENT AND ASSENT

Informed consent is a person's ability to weigh the risks and benefits of participating in research for themselves and to then agree or decline to participate. In many studies, researchers secure this by providing potential participants an information sheet that goes over what they are being asked to do, what the potential risks are, and what the potential benefits are. In a museum setting, it may or may not make sense to prepare a written study information sheet, even though they are commonly mandated by IRBs. When working with people with cognitive disabilities, you should weigh whether you are comfortable having a caregiver consent on the individual's behalf.

Even if someone else consents for the study participant, assent is also crucial. Assent is someone's agreement to participate in a study, even if they are not able to understand all of the risks and benefits. You should garner verbal assent from every study participant. You can do this by explaining the study and its risks and benefits in a way that the participant can understand.

STAKEHOLDER NEEDS

Another important factor is the needs and expectations of stakeholders. For example, many funders may require you to collect evaluation data in exchange for their support. In our case, our program development partners did not request we collect any data beyond the anecdotal, so there was no financial benefit to the organization to collect new data.

Your organization's leaders may also ask for some kind of data confirming the need for accessibility initiatives. This is where turning to medical or advocacy organizations, like Alzheimer's Disease International, may come in handy. For example, according to that group's 2023 research, there are ten million new cases of dementia worldwide every year—and the rate of formal diagnosis ranges from 20 to 50 percent of cases in high-income countries like the United States to even fewer in lower- and middle-income countries.[11] Using this global data, we could make an effective case for offering these programs in our community, not only for those diagnosed with dementia but for everyone who may be experiencing related symptoms.

ALTERNATIVE WAYS OF COLLECTING DATA

If you have determined that collecting data via a survey or interview is not of benefit to your participants, there are other evaluation methods and ways to document successes and identify parts of the program that need improvement. We offer four alternatives for you to consider.

ACCESSIBILITY AUDITS

An accessibility audit invites experts on disabilities (either a community partner and/or someone who is disabled) to visit your site and document accessibility issues and potential violations of the Americans with Disabilities Act (ADA). While we have not done accessibility audits specific to Memory Cafés, we recently had a student advocacy group at our local school for the blind perform one for our whole site at no cost to us. This practice can apply not only to your physical space but to digital venues, like your website, as well. Documenting accessibility issues at your physical and virtual sites is a key step to planning any program effectively—not just accessibility programming.

If you do take this route, we recommend creating an advance plan of what you will do after you receive the audit's results and who will ultimately be responsible for following through on the recommendations. For programs working specifically with individuals with Alzheimer's and/or dementia, an accessibility audit may include metrics that measure whether the program is physically accessible to their needs (e.g., if the program involves walking, standing, or sitting, whether you need to make accommodations for those portions), and whether the program is cognitively appropriate for the participants based on studies and research.

STAFF JOURNALING

Reflective journaling is more common for staff in higher education than in the museum field, but you may find it useful to borrow this practice and have facilitators journal after every program. In a reflective journal, educators write about their interests, curiosities, and experiences to help develop further awareness and understanding.[12] A 2006 study with a cohort of teaching practicum students found that students felt reflective journaling helped them document the issues they were facing, their perceived teaching strengths and weaknesses, and the questions they had.[13] Adopting this model for your accessibility program may help record the program's strengths, areas of improvement, and observed impact on participants, without having to collect data from the participants themselves.

LOOKING FOR SECONDARY RESEARCH AND EVALUATION STUDIES

In some ways, the abundance of preexisting research into the benefits of museum programs for people with dementia is unique. But in other ways it is not. As the other chapters in this book attest, many museums are working to make themselves more accessible, and doing and publishing evaluation studies is a key part of that. This means you should have a considerable body of external research to support your program's impact, no matter what area of accessibility you are working in.

On the topic of Memory Cafés, we found published evaluation studies like one from a government-funded Memory Café initiative in Victoria, Australia, which concluded that the program "provided an opportunity for social inclusion and peer support,"[14] and recommended that the government keep funding the initiative.[15] We also found a lot of scholarly research from the United Kingdom on how museums, particularly art museums, can be beneficial for aging adults. According to a qualitative evaluation of art gallery programs in the UK, the setting provided intellectual stimulation, opportunities for social inclusion, and engagement with the pieces of art for those living with dementia, as well as carer respite and support.[16] A literature review of studies seeking to gauge the benefits of Alzheimer's support groups (of which Memory Cafés are a part) across the United States, UK, and Australia found no conclusive evidence that groups increased participants' "psychosocial outcomes," such as improving mood and enhancing quality of life.[17] However, one study found that people with both early- and middle-stage dementia did have marked improvements in mood after handling objects as a part of a museum program.[18] Another evaluation of a House of Memories program in the UK, a caregivers workshop taking place in a museum, found that participating caregivers became more informed about dementia and experienced the benefits of peer support by participating in the program.[19] A systematic review of evaluations of museum-based dementia programs, again in the UK, uncovered yet another benefit: shared learning.[20] This suggests that while the Memory Café model as a whole has not been researched enough to claim to offer concrete benefits, some of the individual activities that take place during a Conner Prairie Memory Café already have demonstrated positive impacts for the program's participants.

The resources we've cited above and throughout this chapter came from the dedicated work of a graduate student and later an intern (who are both coauthors on this chapter). Their research primarily consisted of conducting literature reviews, which is why we could point to evidence that supported the museum doing the program without collecting data directly from participants. In our experience, a literature review can also be a great way to invite outside voices into your audience research. It can be a short-term, limited-time project for an intern, graduate student, or nonevaluation staff member. Their research can be then synthesized into a short paper that your museum education and development staff alike can cite. We give guidance on conducting your own literature review below.

CONDUCTING A LITERATURE REVIEW

A literature review begins with doing a quick web search to see if there is enough information about the topic you're examining. In the past, we have used Google Scholar because it is easy to navigate, convenient, and only includes published and peer-reviewed academic sources. However, many museum-specific sources are not found in formal academic sources but in blogs or news websites, so a general web search using your preferred search engine is also a good idea.

Once you know there are available resources about your desired topic, it is then time to develop a research question. A research question helps guide your search process and serves as a reminder of the literature review's purpose. The research question can be as open-ended or as specific as you'd like, though this also depends on the availability of the necessary literature in your initial search.

When searching for articles, it is important to start with broad keywords, then get more specific once you have read general articles or find gaps in your research. Before beginning your literature review in earnest, you will want to become familiar with the words that are often used to describe the programming you are looking for. For example, museum programs for people who are neurodivergent or have cognitive disabilities are often called "sensory friendly." Programs for people with dementia at museums can be called "dementia friendly," specifically use the word "Alzheimer's," or have "memory" in the title. Developing a list of useful keywords that you discover as you read through articles and testimonials can help lead you to more sources. See text box 7.1 for more tips on keywords.

As you find sources, you may run into paywalls that prevent you from reading an academic article without paying an exorbitant amount of money (e.g., thirty or fifty dollars) for access. We offer some tips on how to find research articles for free in textbox 7.2.

BOX 7.1. MORE TIPS

We recommend reviewing Boolean operators, which are conjunctions used in a search query to help narrow the search. The most common ones are AND, OR, and NOT. Using AND means the web search will find things that mention both topics. Using OR means that the search will find things that mention either topic or both. Using NOT will help limit your search by searching for one thing while excluding something else. You may also want to use the wildcard symbol (*) in some searches that will find anything that fills in the blank marked by the asterisks. This is extremely helpful when looking for museum sources because you can search for both "museums" and "museum" by searching "museum*." In our case, we started with larger terms like "museum* AND accessibility" and "museum* AND Alzheimer's'." Once you find out about a specific program, like Memory Cafés or MeetMe at MOMA, you can narrow your search by just looking for sources on that particular program.

BOX 7.2. HOW TO FIND RESEARCH THAT IS FREE TO ACCESS

1. Download the Chrome or Firefox extension, Unpaywall, which is free and legal brower extension that allows you to obtain some academic articles.
2. Open Access Button is a website that allows you to search for specific, open access articles. There is also a Chrome and Firefox extension.
3. Directory of Open Access Journals is a website that allows you to search for open access journals and articles. It allows you to search for journals in a variety of academic disciplines.
4. Some journals such as JSTOR and Elsevier have open access sections.
5. Local public and university libraries have access to databases that you can use in-person and have reference librarians that can also request certain articles.
6. Do a survey of your institution's professional memberships. Often-times, professional memberships in the museum field come with access to field-specific journals like *Visitor Studies* or the *Journal of Museum Education.*
7. Get an account on ResearchGate or Academia. Both websites allow academic researchers to upload articles they have published for free. If an article is not available, you have the ability to politely message the author if they have an account and request a copy.

8. University repositories like may also be a good place to find articles (one example is Indiana University's scholarworks: https://scholarworks.iu.edu/dspace/).
9. Browse informalscience.org for evaluation studies from other museums and organizations. Informal Science is a part of the National Science Foundation (NSF), and many summative evaluations of museum exhibits and programs funded by NSF are uploaded at their community repository: https://www.informalscience.org/search-results.

LESSONS LEARNED AND REFLECTIONS

Over time, Memory Cafés have changed at Conner Prairie due to external factors (such as the COVID-19 pandemic) and the internal capacity needed to support the program. The following are our candid reflections on what we have learned from firsthand experience, combined with secondary research and evaluation. These are our recommendations for what to consider for starting an accessibility-oriented program at your institution.

FUNDING AND SPONSORSHIP

Oftentimes, an evaluation's scope is determined by the requests of funders. While our Memory Cafés have primarily been funded out of Conner Prairie's operating budget for the past five years, we have occasionally offset the costs with sponsorship and foundation support. In these cases, anecdotal data and our literature review have given our development staff the supporting evidence they need to fundraise for the program.

Our development staff support the program by looking for companies or organizations whose initiatives align with Memory Cafés. For example, one sponsor is a local business that provides care for individuals suffering from memory loss. Staff have also sought support from foundations for the program, but this has been less successful because foundations' application processes are very competitive and Memory Cafés may be less appealing for funding than other applicants because the number of people they serve is on the lower side.

If your organization has dedicated fundraising staff, it is key to collaborate and work with them to identify potential funding sources for an accessibility program. This helps ensure the longevity of your program. However, remember to consistently advocate for ethical data collection and data use, as per our previous recommendations, as funders can require survey-based data that demonstrates that programs are effective. In our situation, this was not the case.

OPERATIONAL SUPPORT AND SUSTAINABILITY

Since starting the program, we have been able to argue for its continued existence on the program calendar due to its high degree of mission alignment, its low cost of operation, and the secondary research we have identified to confirm the benefits of offering the program. We also recommend that you consider the following when thinking through how the organization can support your program in the long term.

HAVING A DEDICATED TEAM

When the person planning an accessibility program is doing several other jobs at the museum, they can find it hard to dedicate the necessary time to ensure that program is high quality. Unfortunately, like us, you may nonetheless find yourself in this situation. If that is the case, we advise that you hire or restructure roles, if possible, to designate dedicated program staff. A team of staff can help plan the program, build relationships to support it, and get the word out that it is happening. A 2019 literature review of dementia programs in heritage settings in the UK stressed this importance of staffing up so that you can not only adequately plan the program but also support participants and help them feel safe and secure.[21] If you are in the situation of wearing multiple hats at the museum where you work and you want to start an accessibility program, we ask you to think about what you are going to *stop* doing as a result. Pulling in extra hours to make an accessibility program happen is not sustainable long-term. Plus, it sends a message to your organization that accessibility work is something they can keep in the "other duties as assigned" bullet point in somebody's job description instead of hiring dedicated staff that can make the program a sustainable, long-term success.

BUILD RELATIONSHIPS WITH COMMUNITY PARTNERS

At the beginning of this chapter, you read about how community partners first prompted us to create this program. Collaborating with these community partners and involving them in the program's creation was essential for the Memory Cafés' success—it could not have happened without them. We do not recommend that you attempt an accessibility program without a dedicated community partner. Within the disability community, there is a saying: "Nothing about us without us." Involving community partners and stakeholders who belong to the community you want to serve is crucial to creating a well-informed, beneficial program. They can advise you on appropriate language, training, and accessibility audits. They can give you ideas on how to expand your program. From our perspective, the best way to find community partners is to utilize the networking capabilities of your organization's fundraising teams and board members. The leadership members of your organizations are likely to have a large network of connections that could present an amazing partnership opportunity.

PRIORITIZE MARKETING AND AWARENESS-BUILDING

Marketing the program has been the largest challenge for us over time. Because Memory Cafés are for a specific group in the population, marketing them via social media, the museum's website, or the other usual channels does not necessarily result in increases to attendance. We have found the most success sending announcements of new Memory Cafés to community partners that serve people with dementia. But finding and forming those relationships takes time. While you can attempt to encourage your participants to publicize the program via word of mouth, you have much more direct control over the relationships you manage. Effective marketing helps get knowledge of your program out to those who can benefit from it.

COVID-19 AND ADAPTIVE CHANGE TO PROGRAMS

Along with the rest of the world, we had to pivot quite drastically to continue to offer guest experiences during the lockdown period of the COVID-19 pandemic. Alzheimer's and other forms of dementia are already incredibly isolating diseases, so when those individuals had no choice but to self-isolate, it was more important than ever to make sure there was a resource available to them to engage socially with others. Again, we turned to secondary research to educate ourselves about what other organizations were doing with similar programming and inform our decisions. We looked to local assisted living centers' websites and applicable academic journals and articles. Most schools, assisted living communities, adult care centers, and so forth, were relying on virtual experiences for their residents. Zoom, Microsoft Teams, and Google Office were all essential tools to bring virtual programming to communities.

However, this pivot proved more difficult in practice than in planning. Technology can be difficult to navigate for older generations, and sometimes adult care centers and assisted living facilities had trouble getting all of their residents in a room together to participate in the program. So, even though the resources were there, and the intent was to deliver programs to folks from the comfort and safety of their own home or residence, the Impact fell quite short. While we shut down in-person Memory Café programming for a year, we only had three successful virtual Memory Café programs. By "successful," we mean that people tuned into the program; there were quite a few instances when we planned and marketed the programs, but no participants showed up. We also noticed that active guest participation decreased significantly with online programming. Caregivers mentioned that their loved ones didn't feel as comfortable speaking with someone through a computer as they did in person. As we learned in the best practices portion of our training, much of the benefit of the Memory Café program comes with face-to-face, in-person interaction—something that virtual programs just could not do.

EXPANDING AND FUTURE PLANS

If the COVID-19 pandemic taught us anything, it's that you can't necessarily rely on people coming to your site for every program. You also need to meet them where they are. In the near future, we plan to build on our past successes by offering Memory Cafés in more places and formats. We are currently looking at bringing Memory Cafés into assisted living communities. This may require a nominal cost from the facilities, but if we get this expansion sponsored as hoped, we would be able to do it for free. Additionally, we would like to reexamine our staffing model so that we can support and sustain future Memory Cafés through a dedicated team of staff. This would help ensure they serve their intended audience as best they can.

Based on our experiences overall, we would encourage you to look into hosting a Memory Café at your institution. A growing list of museums are beginning to do so, including the Metropolitan Museum of Art, Currier Museum of Art, and the Frye Art Museum in 2023 alone. As we have shown with how we use Memory Cafés to engage across our site, you can use this program format with any museum collection. We feel that museums are uniquely equipped to be successful with it, as we hope we illustrated throughout this chapter. Or, if Memory Cafés are not the model you prefer to use, maybe you will come with the next innovative idea.

THE IMPORTANCE OF SECONDARY RESEARCH AND EVALUATION STUDIES

Hopefully we have also convinced you of the benefits of secondary research and evaluation studies in developing experiential programs for people with cognitive disabilities. After reading the thought process and questions we've posed in this chapter, we hope you will take the time to consider if surveys, interviews, focus groups, and observations are the best evaluation methods for your participants. As you have seen, we have decided that is it not ethical for us in relation to our Memory Café participants, but that does not mean we don't use data to inform our programming. We use literature reviews to constantly monitor the field for new studies and information, like when we were deciding how to proceed with programming during the COVID-19 pandemic. We leave you with this: we urge you to question not just if the program design serves its intended audience but if data collection does too. And when you believe that it

Karen Breece, Kelsey Van Voorst, and Maia Swinson

does not, as we found, we encourage you to look to other ways of knowing we have laid out in this chapter, including continually mining the wealth of secondary evaluation and research studies that are available to practitioners.

NOTES

1. For more on social objects, see Nina Simon, "Chapter 4: Social Objects," in *The Participatory Museum,* https://participatorymuseum.org/chapter4/.
2. Dorthe Berntsen, "Earlier Memories are Relatively Spared in Dementia. Why?" *Psyche*, April 24, 2023. https://psyche.co/ideas/earlier-memories-are-relatively-spared-in-dementia-why
3. For more on MeetMe at MOMA, see "Research and Development," *The MOMA Alzheimer's Project: Making Art Accessible to People with Dementia,* accessed September 8, 2023, https://www.moma.org/visit/accessibility/meetme/resources/#history.
4. "Alzheimer Cafés," Alzheimer's Disease International, accessed September 8, 2023, https://www.alzint.org/what-we-do/policy/dementia-friendly-communities/alzheimer-cafes/.
5. Fabian Hutmacher, "Do You Remember? Similarities and Differences between the Earliest Childhood Memories for the Five Senses," *Memory* 29, no. 3 (2021): 345–52, https://doi.org/10.1080/09658211.2021.1895222.
6. Linda J. Thomson et al., "Effects of a Museum-Based Social Prescription Intervention on Quantitative Measures of Psychological Wellbeing in Older Adults," *Perspectives in Public Health* 138, no. 1 (2018): 28–38, https://doi.org/10.1177/1757913917737563.
7. Paul M. Camic and Helen J. Chatterjee, "Museums and Art Galleries as Partners for Public Health Interventions," *Perspectives in Public Health* 133, no. 1 (2013): 66–71, https://doi.org/10.1177/1757913912468523.
8. Nan Greenwood et al., "A Qualitative Study of Carers' Experiences of Dementia Cafés: A Place to Feel Supported and Be Yourself," *BMC Geriatrics* 17, no. 1 (2017): 164, https://doi.org/10.1186/s12877-017-0559-4.
9. Debbie Kinsey et al., "The Impact of Including Carers in Museum Programmes for People with Dementia: A Realist Review," *Arts & Health* 13, no. 1 (2021): 1–19, https://doi.org/10.1080/17533015.2019.1700536.
10. Katrina Cubit, "Informed Consent for Research Involving People with Dementia: A Grey Area," *Contemporary Nurse* 34, no. 2 (2010): 230–36, https://doi.org/10.5172/conu.2010.34.2.230.
11. "Dementia Statistics," Alzheimer's Disease International, https://www.alzint.org/about/dementia-facts-figures/dementia-statistics/.
12. Teuku Zulfikar and Mujiburrahman, "Understanding Own Teaching: Becoming Reflective Teachers Through Reflective Journals, *International and Multidisciplinary Perspectives* 19, no. 1 (2018): 3
13. Teuku Zulfikar and Mujiburrahman, "Understanding Own Teaching," 11.
14. Briony Dow et al., "Evaluation of Alzheimer's Australia Vic Memory Lane Cafés," *International Psychogeriatrics* 23, no. 2 (2011): 249. doi:10.1017/S1041610210001560.
15. Dow et al., 252.

16. Paul M. Camic et al., "Theorizing How Art Gallery Interventions Impact People With Dementia and Their Caregivers," *The Gerontologist* 56, no. 6 (2016): 1033–41, https://doi.org/10.1093/geront/gnv063.
17. G.VR. Toms et al., "A Systematic Narrative Review of Support Groups for People with Dementia," *International Psychogeriatrics* 27, no. 9 (2015): 1461. doi:10.1017/S1041610215000691.
18. Paul M. Camic et al. "Museum Object Handling: A Health-Promoting Community-Based Activity for Dementia Care," *Journal of Health Psychology* 24, no. 6 (2019): 792. doi: 10.1177/1359105316685899.
19. R. Neiva Ganga and K. M. Wilson, "Valuing Family Carers: The Impact of the House of Memories as a Museum-Led Dementia Awareness Program," *International Journal of Care and Caring* 4, no. 4 (2020): 15–17. https://doi.org/10.1332/23978822 0X15966470811065
20. Monika Sharma and Angela Lee, "Dementia-Friendly Heritage Settings: A Literature Review," *International Journal of Building Pathology and Adaptation* 38, no. 2 (2020): 279–310. https://doi.org/10.1108/IJBPA-01-2019-0005.
21. Monika Sharma and Angela Lee, "Dementia-Friendly Heritage Settings: A Literature Review," *International Journal of Building Pathology and Adaptation* 38, no. 2 (2020): 279–310. https://doi.org/10.1108/IJBPA-01-2019-0005.

Nina Simon, "Chapter 4: Social Objects." In *The Participatory Museum.* 2010. https://participatorymuseum.org/chapter4/.

Linda J. Thomson et al., "Effects of a Museum-Based Social Prescription Intervention on Quantitative Measures of Psychological Wellbeing in Older Adults." *Perspectives in Public Health* 138, no. 1 (2018): 28–38. https://doi .org/10.1177/1757913917737563.

Toms, G. R. et al., "A Systematic Narrative Review of Support Groups for People with Dementia," *International Psychogeriatrics* 27, no. 9 (2015): 1439–65. doi:10.1017/S1041610215000691.

Teuku Zulfikar and Mujiburrahman. "Understanding Own Teaching: Becoming Reflective Teachers Through Reflective Journals. *International and Multidisciplinary Perspectives* 19, no. 1 (2018): 3. https://doi.org/10.1080/14623943.2017.1295933

BIBLIOGRAPHY

"Alzheimer Cafés," Alzheimer's Disease International. Accessed September 8, 2023. https://www.alzint.org/what-we-do/policy/dementia-friendly-communities/alzhei mer-Cafés/.

Berntsen, Dorthe. "Earlier Memories are Relatively Spared in Dementia. Why?" *Psyche.* April 24, 2023.https://psyche.co/ideas/earlier-memories-are-relatively -spared-in-dementia-why.

Camic, Paul M., and Helen J. Chatterjee. "Museums and Art Galleries as Partners for Public Health Interventions." *Perspectives in Public Health* 133, no. 1 (2013): 66–71. https://doi.org/10.1177/1757913912468523.

Camic, Paul M. et al. "Theorizing How Art Gallery Interventions Impact People with Dementia and Their Caregivers." *The Gerontologist* 56, no. 6 (2016): 1033–41, https://doi.org/10.1093/geront/gnv063.

Camic, Paul M. et al. "Museum Object Handling: A Health-Promoting Community-Based Activity for Dementia Care." *Journal of Health Psychology* 24, no. 6 (2019): 792. doi: 10.1177/1359105316685899.

Cubit, Katrina. "Informed Consent for Research Involving People with Dementia: A Grey Area." *Contemporary Nurse* 34, no. 2 (2010): 230–36. https://doi.org/10.5172/conu.2010.34.2.230.

"Dementia Statistics." Alzheimer's Disease International. https://www.alzint.org/about/dementia-facts-figures/dementia-statistics/.

Dow, Briony et al. "Evaluation of Alzheimer's Australia Vic Memory Lane Cafés." *International Psychogeriatrics* 23, no. 2 (2011): 249.

Ganga, Rafaela Neiva, and Kerry Wilson. 'Valuing Family Carers: The Impact of House of Memories as a Museum-led Dementia Awareness Programme." *International Journal of Care and Caring* 4, no. 4 (2020): 573–93. https://doi.org/10.1332/239788220X15966470811065

Greenwood, Nan et al. "A Qualitative Study of Carers' Experiences of Dementia Cafés: A Place to Feel Supported and Be Yourself." *BMC Geriatrics* 17, no. 1 (2017): 164. https://doi.org/10.1186/s12877-017-0559-4.

Hutmacher, Fabian. "Do You Remember? Similarities and Differences between the Earliest Childhood Memories for the Five Senses." *Memory* 29, no. 3 (2021): 345–52. https://doi.org/10.1080/09658211.2021.1895222.

Kinsey, Debbie et al. "The Impact of Including Carers in Museum Programmes for People with Dementia: A Realist Review." *Arts & Health* 13, no. 1 (2021): 1–19. https://doi.org/10.1080/17533015.2019.1700536.

"Research and Development." *The MOMA Alzheimer's Project: Making Art Accessible to People with Dementia.* Accessed September 8, 2023. https://www.moma.org/visit/accessibility/meetme/resources/#history.

Sharma, Monika and Lee, Angela. "Dementia-friendly Heritage Settings: A Research Review," *International Journal of Building Pathology and Adaptation*, 38, no. 2 (2020): 279–310. https://doi.org/10.1108/IJBPA-01-2019-0005.

8

The Deaf Culture Project

SETTING AN EXPECTATION OF ADAPTABILITY

Alyssa Carr

The Nelson-Atkins Museum of Art began working with partners in the d/ Deaf and hard-of-hearing community in 2015, when it hosted its first Deaf Culture Day, which has since expanded into an annual Deaf Cultural Festival offering a day of performances, art, and more. Then, in 2017, the museum was awarded a Museums for America Community Anchors grant from the Institute of Museum and Library Services (IMLS) to conduct the Deaf Culture Project, designed to invest in more access resources and increase collaboration with our community partners: the Kansas School for the Deaf, the Museum of Deaf History Arts and Culture, and The Whole Person.

Despite our preexisting relationships with these partners, the staff and volunteers involved in the project came to realize how much we still had to learn about—and from—the d/Deaf and hard-of-hearing community in order to create accessible programming. This chapter describes how the museum leaned into this challenge, prioritizing staff learning and capacity building and championing partner-driven, evaluation-led decision making.

Because a major part of the project involved consulting with experts in ac- commodations for d/Deaf and hard-of-hearing people, we hired a program co- ordinator who was a member of that community, Lucy Crabtree, and contracted with Garibay Group, a firm that specializes in culturally responsive equitable evaluations, to serve as an adviser and conduct a summative evaluation. We then recruited representatives from our existing community partners to serve on an advisory panel that would consult throughout the project and beyond. With the help of this panel, we were able to implement reflective practices,[1] which emphasize self-examination and ongoing learning, and develop several new accessible products and activities through the project.

As a result of the project, the museum began to use Communication Access Realtime Translation captioning (also known as CART, or sometimes "live" or "real-time" captioning) for programming, lectures, and webinars.[2] We hired art teachers whose primary form of communication was American Sign Language (ASL) and implemented monthly in-person and virtual ASL tours, led directly in the language rather than translated from voice. With guidance from partner feedback, we created ASL vlogs (video blogs) featuring staff and community members introducing visitors to the museum and galleries, and video guides narrating artworks in the museum collection in ASL. We created a teacher advisory board comprised entirely of teachers for d/Deaf and hard-of-hearing students. Most importantly, thanks to feedback from our partners, we began to place more emphasis on the Deaf Cultural Festival as a focal point for engagement.

THE MUSEUM AND ITS SHUTTLECOCKS

The Nelson-Atkins is an encyclopedic art museum located in Kansas City, Missouri. It currently maintains collections of more than forty thousand works of art—with well-known highlights including an expansive Asian art collection and four giant shuttlecock sculptures on the museum's lawn. Created by Claes Oldenburg and Coosje van Bruggen, this work casts the museum building itself as a massive badminton net, with the shuttlecocks arranged as if they have landed on either side of the net midgame. Since their installation in 1994, the shuttlecocks have become so iconic that they have become a visual representation of Kansas City itself, appearing on anything from signs and original artworks to t-shirts and drinkware.

Figure 8.1. Image of the Nelson-Atkins Museum with one of the four giant shuttlecocks created by Claes Oldenburg and Coosje van Bruggen on the lawn in front of the museum. *Nelson-Atkins Media Services, Mark McDonald.* *©2015 The Nelson Gallery Foundation.*

Figure 8.2. Nelson-Atkins Museum of Art logo and ASL sign
Design ©2023 The Nelson Gallery Foundation

Because of this symbolic status, the shuttlecocks became the inspiration for one aspect of the Deaf Culture Project: the design of the museum's first-ever ASL sign. Partners and staff developed a playful design riffing on the installation, with one hand held parallel to the body and the other vertically, the fingers fanned out to create the feathers of a shuttlecock.

Figure 8.3. Jackie Niekamp demonstrates the sign for the Nelson-Atkins Museum of Art. Partners and staff used the shuttlecocks as inspiration to create a brand-new sign to represent the Nelson-Atkins Museum of Art: one hand is held parallel to the body while the other hand is held vertically with fingers fanned out to create the feathers of a shuttlecock. *Nelson-Atkins Media Services, Mark McDonald. ©2023 The Nelson Gallery Foundation.*

ACCESS PROGRAMS AT THE NELSON-ATKINS MUSEUM OF ART

While the Deaf Culture Project allowed the Nelson-Atkins to deepen its work in the area considerably, the museum's documented history of access programs stretches back thirty years. Currently, the manager of community and access programs, Jackie Niekamp, partners with more than thirty organizations to provide equitable and inclusive programming for historically marginalized and underrepresented audiences. Community lies at the heart of this access programming; it is important to us to prioritize representation and diversity through exhibitions, artists, and programming. We offer free programs offsite in community centers, onsite at the museum, and virtually over Zoom and Microsoft Teams, creating multiple access points for inclusive experiences. The goals of community and access programs are to ensure that visitors fully experience the museum's exhibitions, programs, and resources; improve their well-being; and feel welcome and respected in the museum.

Some of the audiences we serve through these programs include people facing economic barriers to participation, immigrants and refugees, and people with disabilities. Participants span all ages, from preschool students to older adults. Some examples of current on-site access programs include customized art classes, citizenship preparation classes, studio classes for children and adults on the autism spectrum, special hours and activities for visitors who want low-sensory experiences, tactile tours for visitors who are blind or partially sighted, and gallery tours in partnership with the KU Alzheimer's Disease Research Center and the Alzheimer's Association for those with memory loss and their care partners. Offsite community programs include art-making lessons with skill building in literacy for English language learners, and creative aging classes for adults fifty-five and older.

In addition to these access programs, the Nelson-Atkins holds free annual festivals throughout the year to celebrate diverse cultures, including the Deaf Cultural Festival, Lunar New Year, Passport to India, Juneteenth, Native American Cultural Celebration, and Dia de los Muertos. Each festival celebrates a different culture by devoting an entire day to performances, demonstrations, music, dancing, and artmaking. In 2017 and 2018, we conducted evaluation of each of these cultural festivals, and the museum regularly evaluates all access programs, researching if the museum has met its goals, where it can improve, if guests are satisfied with their experiences, and what options for future programming may be.

THE DEAF CULTURE PROJECT

Funded by a three-year grant from IMLS, the Deaf Culture Project was designed by Community and Access Programs and Evaluation staff with input from partners in the d/Deaf and hard-of-hearing community. It was designed as a suite of interrelated products and activities to provide quality, accessible programs for visitors who are d/Deaf or hard of hearing. The goals of the Deaf Culture Project were to

- Build engagement and learning among visitors who are d/Deaf or hard of hearing.
- Empower community members to fully access, enjoy, and understand the museum's collections and programs.
- Increase the perception of the museum as an accessible and inclusive community resource where everyone feels welcome and respected.
- Build capacity among museum staff and volunteers to positively engage with members of the d/Deaf and hard-of-hearing communities.

It is important to note that the terminology I use to write about people who are d/Deaf or hard of hearing in this chapter reflects nuances in individual identities among the broader community.[3] Throughout the chapter, I use a lowercase d and the term "hard of hearing" to reflect those who do not identify as culturally Deaf, such as people with partial hearing or late-onset deafness, who often see themselves as "culturally hearing" people who happen to have hearing loss. I use an uppercase D to reflect people who are culturally Deaf, meaning they identify with the language, values, history, and art that are unique to Deaf culture. When writing broadly about all individuals with some level of hearing disability, I combine all three terms as "d/Deaf or hard of hearing."

In the beginning phases of the Deaf Culture Project, the museum hired a coordinator of Deaf culture programs fluent in ASL to oversee the logistics of partnerships and programs, Lucy Crabtree. It was Lucy's insight and questions that led to the museum revisiting some previous expectations and assumptions. For example, the original grant stated that "the project [would] benefit visitors who are Deaf, the broader Deaf community (family and friends, sign language interpreters, and organizations that serve people who are Deaf); KSD teachers and students; hearing visitors; NAMA staff and volunteers; the broader museum field." With Lucy's feedback, however, it became clear that, when crafting the proposal, the museum had not considered visitors who are deaf or hard of hearing but do not consider themselves part of the Deaf community.

Though the museum had begun the project with set goals in mind, we readily shifted these to adjust to new information like this and embody a concept of meaningful inclusion, which is often exemplified by the phrase "nothing about us without us."[4] By bringing in Lucy's perspective and pairing it with feedback from community partners and focus groups, we were able to adapt our plans to better represent the people we were attempting to serve. Evaluation activities that took place over the next three years included formative evaluations of festivals, focus groups, posttraining surveys, interviews, multiple partner feedback sessions,

BOX 8.1.

"I joined the Deaf Culture Project at the Nelson-Atkins Museum of Art in January 2018. I almost didn't apply for the position of coordinator, Deaf cultural programs. As someone who is hard of hearing, I expected an initiative named the 'Deaf Culture Project' to be applicable only to people who considered themselves culturally Deaf. What could I possibly bring to the table? However, no fewer than ten friends and acquaintances—many of whom were Deaf or hard of hearing themselves—encouraged me to apply for the job. During the interview process, I answered questions about how to foster an inclusive environment for both culturally Deaf and nonculturally deaf/hard-of-hearing visitors. I was pleasantly surprised to learn how committed the Nelson-Atkins staff was to inclusion and that the Deaf Culture Project was open to casting a wide net for visitors all along the hearing loss spectrum." —Lucy Crabtree, coordinator, Deaf Cultural Programs

Figure 8.4. Lucy Crabtree, Coordinator of Deaf Culture Programs gives an ASL tour of the Bloch Impressionist Galleries during the 2019 Deaf Cultural Day, September 28, 2019, at The Nelson-Atkins Museum of Art in Kansas City, MO
Nelson-Atkins Media Services, Jason Tracy. ©2019 The Nelson Gallery Foundation.

Alyssa Carr

BOX 8.2.

The grant application submitted called for: "American Sign Language (ASL) videos with captioning and audio for fifty objects in the museum collection delivered on iPad minis or downloadable on one's own mobile device; five vlogs (video blogs) for the museum's website, featuring the coordinator, Deaf Culture Programs, using ASL to introduce visitors to the museum and its collection; an orientation and professional development workshops for teachers at the Kansas School for the Deaf (KSD); interactive tours for KSD students and drop-in tours for adults led by gallery guides, Deaf Culture Programs; an annual Deaf Cultural Day with activities and programs that increase awareness of and celebrate Deaf culture; NAMA staff training and the production of three to five vlogs to ensure that future museum staff and volunteers have the skills, knowledge, and resources to effectively serve people who are Deaf.

partner participatory analysis, festival summative evaluations, and interviews and focus groups with museum core teams, partners, and festival performers.

EVALUATION AND ADAPTABILITY

The museum committed to conducting formative evaluations—which take place in the beginning stages of a project to gather feedback on its goals—to ensure that our partners and community members could share their reactions early in the project. This set an expectation of adaptability that would carry on throughout the project. Thanks in large part to our supportive leadership, we were able to develop an environment that welcomed reflective practice, assuring the museum team and our partners that any plans could easily be adapted as needed. We also benefited from a second grant we received from the IMLS during the same time period, through its Museums Empowered program, which allowed the museum to focus on evaluation capacity building while conducting new audience research. This capacity building included educating all museum staff, particularly division directors, about the skills needed to implement, interpret, and apply audience research to strategic decision making. Division leaders, including the museum director, Julián Zugazagoitia, participated in on-site visitor intercepts and learned the methodology behind them. As leadership gained a more nuanced understanding of the evaluation process, they embraced feedback, remained receptive to adaptation, and readily implemented changes as they unfolded—priming them to welcome the Deaf Culture Project's reflective approach.

In spring 2018, we conducted formative evaluation in the form of a series of four focus groups. We held two of these focus groups with educators in the Kansas City area who work with students who are d/Deaf or hard of hearing, and two with adults from the area who identify as d/Deaf or hard of hearing themselves. To ensure equity in the evaluation process, we compensated all participants for their time.

Prior to conducting the focus groups, Lucy worked with evaluation staff to determine the most accessible way to structure them. We started from a foundation of universal design—"the design and composition of an environment so that it can be accessed, understood and used to the greatest extent possible by all people regardless of their age, size, ability or disability"[5]—and expanded from there to ensure an accessible environment for communication. Below are some communication tips that were very useful during participatory feedback sessions and focus groups:

- Ensure that only one person speaks at a time.
- Raise a hand or give another visual cue if you would like to be heard.
- Ensure that everyone is visible to each other, with the room well-lit and seating in rounds rather than classroom style.
- Ask participants to engage in only one activity at a time, including dedicated time for notetaking.
- Ensure that video and audio sources are captioned or transcribed in real time.
- Dedicate resources for live captioning and hiring interpreters and provide as much material in text as possible.
- Most importantly, ask attendees to either talk *or* look, never to do both at once.

EDUCATOR FOCUS GROUPS

For our first category of focus groups, we relied on our community partners and members of our existing teacher advisory board to recruit educators of d/Deaf and hard-of-hearing students throughout the Kansas City metro region. A total of eleven teachers participated in the two focus group sessions, which explored their existing connections to and perceptions of the museum, both professionally and personally. They discussed the perceived value of informal learning or field trip experiences, student needs, and their own professional development needs and interests. They also provided feedback and recommendations on our proposals for teacher professional development, tours and field trips, and our plans to hire five on-call ASL tour guides.

The results of the discussion provided a prime example of the importance of evaluation—as we learned we had made a lot of incorrect assumptions in our original grant narrative! Originally, we had planned to focus on professional

Alyssa Carr

development workshops for educators, but we learned during the focus groups that teachers were less interested in directed professional development than social engagement with other teachers of d/Deaf or hard-of-hearing students in the area. They shared that they often feel isolated on a day-to-day basis and welcomed the opportunity to get together with others in their position.

They also shared that they were concerned with our proposal for tours and field trip experiences because their past experiences with field trips had been overwhelming due to insufficient accessibility support at the host sites. As one teacher commented, "I, as a hearing teacher, have brought kids and had to go places, and I have to become the interpreter, which is frustrating because I still have to supervise and classroom-manage and expound on things to try and make forced connections, but I can't do those well because I'm having to interpret. And so that's always a struggle on field trips for me."

Furthermore, they were concerned about visual split attention, which occurs when students are required to take in multiple sources of visual information at the same time, such as ASL interpretation and a performance.[6] This creates a situation where students may not be able to process all the information that they are required to in the time given. One teacher explained this using an example of watching a play: "Let's say if you have the interpreter sitting over at the side, you know, far away from the action, you'll look at the actor . . . see what they're doing . . . but what are they saying? You have to look over at the interpreter, get the message . . . Then you're missing the acting as it's happening. Then you look back and miss what the interpreter's saying, so it's exhausting on the eyes. In the beginning, you're watching, then you start to go, 'Uh, whatever.'"

To combat visual split attention during our proposed field trips or tours, teachers provided a few tips:

1. Set communication expectations at the start.
2. Allow only one person to speak at a time.
3. Raise your hand or give some other visual cue for attention.
4. Ensure everyone is visible to each other so students do not miss comments from their peers.
5. Most importantly, ask participants to talk or look, never both at the same time.

The educators also provided feedback on our plans for staffing our new ASL tours. At the time of the project in 2018, the Nelson-Atkins provided all tours on a drop-in basis, rather than prescheduled arrangements. To offer the same drop-in availability to d/Deaf or hard-of-hearing audiences, we proposed hiring five on-call tour guides fluent in ASL. However, the educators told us they would prefer we hire one part-time educator instead, which would provide a stable job for someone who is d/Deaf or hard of hearing and give the children

Figure 8.5. Micki Keck, community partner, gives an ASL tour during the 2018 Deaf Cultural Festival. *Nelson-Atkins Media Services, Jason Tracy. ©2019 The Nelson Gallery Foundation.*

and students on the tours the benefit of seeing a positive role model in the position. One educator commented, "I like those d/Deaf-friendly, d/Deaf-aware places that I frequent. If there's a d/Deaf adult that works there, I'm there every year with every group, because not only do you have direct communication, but you also have a d/Deaf adult that's employed as a role model for those kids."

The teachers shared an amazing wealth of information with us. In providing their expertise and sharing their experiences and suggestions, they helped us rethink our activities and redesign them based on community input.

COMMUNITY MEMBER FOCUS GROUPS

For our second category of focus groups, we recruited twenty d/Deaf and hard-of-hearing adults through our partner organizations, who met in two separate groups. The first group consisted of those who identify as Deaf, and the second consisted of those who identify as deaf, hard of hearing, or children of deaf adults (CODA). We invited the participants to share their perspectives and reflect on the Deaf Culture Project proposal. Their feedback informed several changes to the proposal, all of which strengthened our offerings and created stronger connections to the d/Deaf community. In particular, we learned more about the nuances between d/Deaf and hard-of-hearing identities that I discussed earlier in this chapter, and how those differences impacted our proposed programming.

During the focus groups, we learned that many people who are late-deaf-ened or hard of hearing do not consider themselves to be part of Deaf culture or community, even if they know some ASL or other sign language. Therefore, an emphasis on that culture or community in accessibility and inclusion efforts, such as our Deaf Cultural Festival, deters some people who could benefit from participating. Some participants had never even heard of the festival or other accessibility options at the museum. Learning this, we realized that we needed to update our marketing and make it clear that the Deaf Cultural Festival is for everyone. These changes included hiring more well-known d/Deaf and hard-of-hearing performers and artists and ensuring event marketing more accurately reflected the diverse range of experiences the festival encompasses. This also served as an important reminder that accessibility and inclusion is truly not one-size-fits-all—not even within one community—and that we need to make sure that we don't think of disability categories as monolithic.

Several focus group participants also admitted they considered the museum a "hearing people place." Their logic was that so many museums offer audio guides, which they cannot participate in. They also shared stories of public venues where their requests for accommodations were ignored or were insufficient for their full participation. They assumed that the Nelson-Atkins would be similar, and, thus, not for them.

They then weighed in on the plan for ASL video guides in our original grant proposal, which called for producing a total of fifty guides. At first, the participants were not very enthusiastic about the idea of video guides in general, preferring in-person ASL tours provided by fluent museum staff to app-based ASL interpretation of single artworks. They were more convinced after we showed them a video example from the Whitney Museum of American Art,[7] though they felt that fewer, higher-quality ASL video guides using d/Deaf actors who are native ASL users would be better than more of lower quality. In the end, we produced thirty-one ASL video guides instead of the originally proposed fifty.

On the other hand, they were immediately excited about our plans to produce ASL vlogs to introduce website visitors to our collection. They viewed the vlogs as an effective way to reach the wider community and market the Deaf Culture Project and festival—both to hearing and d/Deaf or hard-of-hearing audiences. Originally, the proposal called for producing five of these vlogs, but based on the enthusiastic response, as well as the decision to reduce the number of ASL video guides, we increased this number. Ultimately, we created fourteen vlogs through the project, which we shared on the Nelson-Atkins website and YouTube channel and played continuously in the museum lobby. We used some of these vlogs specifically to market the Deaf Cultural Festival and reach a wider audience than traditional marketing could.[8]

About half of our participants in these focus groups were not native or fluent ASL users, which served as an important reminder that not everyone

Matisse combines rich color and lively patterns.

Figure 8.6. Screen capture of ASL Video Guide describing "Lady Seated Before a Black Background" by Henri Matisse.

Still image from Smartify ASL video, courtesy of The Nelson-Atkins Museum of Art. Displayed artwork: Henri Matisse (French, 1869–1954). Woman Seated before a Black Background, 1942. Oil on canvas, 21¾ x 18¼ inches (55.2 x 46.4 cm). The Nelson-Atkins Museum of Art, Kansas City, Missouri. Gift of Henry W. and Marion H. Bloch, 2015.13.13. Art © Succession H. Matisse / Artists Rights Society (ARS), New York.
Photo courtesy Nelson-Atkins Media Services.

with hearing loss knows sign language or will benefit from an ASL interpreter. We found that providing both ASL interpretation and CART captioning was necessary to enable full participation in our evaluation. The participants also emphasized the need for captioning during general-public events, which led us to incorporate live CART captioning in our exhibitions and events going forward. Studies have shown that this does not just benefit those who are d/Deaf or hard of hearing, but many other people, such as those who are learning to read, learning a new language, or who have auditory processing issues.[9]

CAPACITY-BUILDING, STAFF TRAINING, AND EVALUATION

Capacity building and staff and volunteer training took place in August 2018. It was organized by the Coordinator of Deaf Programs and our partner organization the Whole Person. While the training focused on deaf-friendly awareness and practices, it also discussed disability etiquette in general. It emphasized using person-first language, such as saying "a person with a disability," rather than "a disabled person." It also stressed the importance of allowing each person you interact with to guide the interaction. While this may seem obvious, it

Alyssa Carr

helped staff and volunteers remember that each person, regardless of ability, has their own likes and dislikes in how they prefer to be approached.

The training then moved onto best practices for interacting with people who are d/Deaf or hard of hearing specifically. This started with dispelling a few myths surrounding hearing loss—such as that everyone who experiences it is a lip reader or uses sign language—and emphasizing that the best thing to do is to ask someone their preferences. A few key tips for speaking with people who are d/Deaf or hard of hearing the training shared were:

- Face the person when you are speaking and listening.
- Make eye contact.
- Do not exaggerate your speech, speak too slowly or too fast, mumble, look away, whisper, cover your mouth, or speak while eating.
- If the person you are talking to cannot understand you, try rephrasing what you are saying, or write notes back and forth.

When communicating via writing, you can use either a pen or pencil and paper, or the notes function on a smartphone. If the person indicates that they prefer ASL, and you know even a little, use it. Even if you feel shy or diffident about your ability, you should not worry, as people will likely appreciate your effort regardless. If you would like to learn some basic signs and common phrases, you can use smartphone apps to pick them up quickly, such as *The ASL App*.[10] When working with a sign language interpreter, it is important to talk directly to the person you are conversing with and not the interpreter. Trust that the person and the interpreter will either position themselves as they need or tell you what they need. Be mindful of where they are located so that you can keep sightlines open.

Just after the 2018 training, we conducted a retrospective pre/post survey with staff and volunteers who participated. Those who attended the training reported that they had a higher rate of awareness afterward and could identify specific tips and strategies for communication. When asked what ideas they took away from the training, one respondent stated, "I have been reflecting a lot on 'people first' language, how deaf-friendly our educational programs are, and how our spaces at the museum can be more accessible."

We surveyed these staff and volunteers again in 2021 to determine the impact the training had two years later. More than half of attendees reported that they had used what they learned in that time, with some saying their overall comfort level serving visitors in the d/Deaf and hard-of-hearing communities had increased. However, most respondents said they were still not fully comfortable interacting with these visitors. The majority also said they had not discussed what they learned during the training with colleagues since it took place. Furthermore, only 45 percent of those who completed the first survey in 2018 completed the second in 2021. Although we attribute some of these disappointing findings to the COVID-19 pandemic, which prevented staff from practicing what they learned to some extent, we also concluded that all future trainings should be followed up with shorter refresher trainings to help attendees practice. One attendee articulated this in a comment on the survey: "I would like to have regular tips or reminders . . . because it was a long time ago that we did this. Also, we have new colleagues that could benefit from this training too."

2018 DEAF CULTURAL FESTIVAL EVALUATION

The 2018 Deaf Cultural Festival was the perfect opportunity to establish a baseline of visitor perceptions from those who attended the festival. We designed a survey to learn the demographics of who was attending the festival, how many attendees identified as d/Deaf or hard of hearing, what activities and experiences offered they liked the best, their overall satisfaction with the festival, and their agreement with questions about increased awareness of d/Deaf and hard-of-hearing culture and experiences. When crafting questions for the survey, we consulted an expert in d/Deaf identity to provide

Figure 8.7. Festival visitors to the 2018 Deaf Cultural Festival. An adult and child discuss what they want to eat, salad or chicken. *Nelson-Atkins Media Services; Jason Tracy.* *©2018 The Nelson Gallery Foundation.*

edits and feedback about how to phrase questions. For example, we phrased the identity question as, "Do you identify as Deaf, deaf, hard of hearing, or late-deafened?" making sure to reflect as many potential members of the d/Deaf community as possible.

To field the survey, we deployed volunteer data collectors to the festival, all of whom had attended the deaf-friendly awareness training. They were equipped with copies of the survey, a laminated survey request form, and notepads and pencils for quick questions and answers with visitors as needed. If a visitor indicated they needed visual communication, data collectors would hand them the request form, which described the study and asked if they would be willing to participate. This approach worked well, and a total of ninety-four visitors participated in the survey.

The data showed that the majority of respondents found out about the festival through word of mouth, and close to 80 percent were attending their first festival at the Nelson-Atkins. Most (71 percent) stated that they were not themselves d/Deaf or hard of hearing but were connected to the community in some way, including through family members, friends, or employment as ASL students, teachers, and interpreters. Twenty percent identified as d/Deaf or hard of hearing themselves.

After the festival, internal evaluators traveled to partner locations to do community-based participatory data analysis, which allows partners to participate in the research process as coanalysts and cointerpreters of the data.[11] This important step showed partners that we wanted their perspectives about what results meant and how to emphasize them. As the analyst on staff at the museum, I put together descriptive statistics, charts, and tables to share with our partners. During the meetings, we projected these charts and tables on a large screen while we sat together to determine what was of most interest to them and what findings they would like more information about. (For others conducting this type of participatory analysis, this could also be accomplished in a data "walk" or "placemat" format, where the facilitator places posters of findings around the room and encourages participants to indicate their interest in specific data by applying sticker dots on charts that intrigue them.) Interpreters assisted with translation, and we extended the meeting time to allow for looking at and digesting the data before discussion. Our partners expressed their interest in, and inquired about the effectiveness of, activities and experiences to inform the planning of the upcoming festival. For the 2019 festival, they were particularly interested in artmaking activities and workshops with an artist working in Deaf View/Image Art (De'VIA)—which examines and expresses the Deaf experience from a cultural, linguistic, and intersectional point of view[12]—and hosting more nationally known performers, both of which came to fruition.

Figure 8.8. Promotion of Deaf Culture Festival. *Design ©2023 The Nelson Gallery Foundation*

PRIORITY SETTING WITH STAKEHOLDERS

The museum brought on the Garibay Group, headed by Cecilia Garibay, to conduct certain evaluation activities throughout the lifespan of the project, such as the survey about the deaf awareness staff training mentioned earlier. We selected the Garibay Group as the external evaluator of the project because it specializes in culturally responsive equitable evaluation, which prioritizes a focal community's authority and sovereignty.[13] During the beginning phases of the Garibay team's evaluation, they worked with the museum to develop four priority areas, including assessing the following:

1. The value of the project for the d/Deaf and hard-of-hearing communities
2. The nature and quality of our community collaboration

Alyssa Carr

3. The overall success of the 2020 Deaf Cultural Festival
4. The extent to and ways in which the project built staff capacity

Before getting to these tasks, the very first priority for the Garibay Group was to gather all stakeholders in a room for a priority-setting session. This took place in May of 2018, after the focus groups with educators and community members occurred—a decision we made partially due to scheduling constraints and partially to allow the full group to discuss the focus group feedback. During the session, we identified further adjustments to the program beyond those the focus group participants had suggested, as learnings went both ways. For example, while the museum had put its festivals on the backburner at the time, wanting to emphasize evergreen initiatives instead, we learned during this session that the Deaf Cultural Festival was a much higher priority to the community than we had initially realized. We also heard the desire from community members to see national performers at the festival. Both of these findings led us to shift more resources to the festival than we had originally planned. This required us to work through tensions that emerged in cultural norms and practices and ultimately to adjust our goals and planned deliverables.

In all of its projects, the Garibay Group emphasizes flexibility and encourages the museums it partners with to take time for reflective practice throughout. This flexibility was an asset in our case, considering all of the shifts we made to our goals and priorities, as well as those imposed by the COVID-19

Figure 8.9. Visitors cheering for a performance during the 2018 Deaf Cultural Festival.
Nelson-Atkins Media Services, Jason Tracy. ©2017 The Nelson Gallery Foundation.

pandemic, which hit midway through the project. Cecilia emphasized examining the equity of our practices and progress we were making throughout the phases of the project, not just at the end.

SUMMATIVE EVALUATION OF THE 2020 DEAF CULTURAL FESTIVAL

We scheduled a second full analysis of the Deaf Cultural Festival for 2020. However, due to COVID-19, we ended up having to move the festival to an entirely virtual format, with content offered on the museum website for a month. Because of this format change, we saw fewer numbers of people "attend" the festival. Even so, the Garibay Group was still able to conduct interviews and surveys. Respondents said they were satisfied overall with the festival and found the quality of the event high. The most popular content on the website was an ASL Slam video. (The full table of view/scroll rates for festival content appears figure 8.10.) When asked what they enjoyed most about the festival, one participant said, "The professional renditions of the stories and the artwork. Please keep this website active as it is such a wonderful resource for (D)deaf students. This can bring them such inspiration as they grow up into their own life dreams."

As part of the summative evaluation (which occurs after a program is finished), we conducted community partner interviews and surveys. The results of these showed that partners felt the museum successfully fostered an atmosphere of feedback and sharing—taking into account partner ideas for the Deaf Cultural Festival and interpreting early focus group and survey findings. They also felt that the Deaf Cultural Festival built community among d/Deaf and hard-of-hearing attendees, celebrated Deaf culture, and increased awareness of Deaf culture for hearing visitors. However, they noted that more work needs to be done to reach more people. One partner noted, "It achieved the goals for those who are coming, but I would like to see more people attending within the Deaf community."

AS THE GRANT ENDED

As the project came to a close, community partner concerns centered around the longevity of the activities and how to expand our partnerships. They expressed a desire for the next phases of the partnership to expand beyond the walls of the museum by offering programming in the community. One partner stated, "If a hearing museum wants to represent a culture, they have to come and participate in that culture and be in that community." They were also concerned about the fact that Lucy's position as coordinator of Deaf culture programs was not renewed at the end of the project, as additional funding to retain her position after the completion of the grant was not available. As one partner said, "There was a real sense of anxiety about a loss of representation

Viewed 25%
43%

Viewed 50%
32%

Viewed 75%
21%

Viewed 100%
4%

Figure 8.10. Screen capture of Google Analytics scroll depth for Deaf Cultural Festival 2020
Nelson-Atkins Museum of Art

Figure 8.11. Visitors asking questions during an ASL tour for the Deaf Awareness Week education event and tour on September 20, 2015, at the Nelson-Atkins Museum of Art in Kansas City, Missouri. *Nelson-Atkins Media Services, Kevin Anderson. ©2015 The Nelson Gallery Foundation.*

at the museum and not having a member of the d/Deaf and hard of hearing community working at the institution . . . because that's part of the reason for the authentic programming that resulted." These concerns are valid and provide a good example of the continued work that needs to be done to maintain access programs and partnerships over the long run.

The Nelson-Atkins used five visitor strategies in support of the Deaf Culture Project: the Deaf Cultural Festival, live captioning, vlogs, ASL video guides, and on-site ASL gallery tours. Garibay Group's summative evaluation of the entire project found that of these five strategies, the Deaf Cultural Festival and live captioning were the most successful and popular among visitors and partners. All of the strategies have continued since the project ended, though we are now offering ASL tours by request instead of on a drop-in basis. Garibay Group found that the Deaf Culture Project resulted in a productive collaboration by building upon and strengthening existing community relationships. The team suggested strategies for continued engagement, including holding more events for and with the d/Deaf and hard-of-hearing communities, collecting art by Deaf artists, and attending community events hosted by partner organizations.

Alyssa Carr

Figure 8.12. A museum docent giving a tour of the Bloch Impressionist Galleries with a sign language interpreter during the 2017 Deaf Cultural Festival.
Nelson-Atkins Media Services, Jason Tracy. ©2017 The Nelson Gallery Foundation.

SETTING AN EXPECTATION OF ADAPTABILITY

Making evaluation accessible is not as easy as consulting a checklist and implementing accommodations, but this was—and is—crucial to our successes. Reaching out to the community through surveys and focus groups, and using data to engage in conversations, allowed us to understand where we needed to grow, leading to meaningful connections with our community. Evaluation facilitated sustained communication and openness to learning, which allowed the Nelson-Atkins to partner successfully with community organizations and improve our offerings for the d/Deaf and hard-of-hearing communities. And it was through evaluation and listening to experts, like Lucy, that the museum was able to adjust programing throughout the life of the project and prioritize our partners.

NOTES

1. Bernadette T. Lynch (2011) Custom-made Reflective Practice: Can Museums Realise Their Capabilities in Helping Others Realise Theirs?, *Museum Management and Curatorship*, 26(5), 441-458, doi: 10.1080/09647775.2011.621731, pp. 441-44
2. "Real-Time Captioning (CART)." Deaf and Hard of Hearing, August 30, 2022. https://mn.gov/deaf-hard-of-hearing/communication-access/cart/.

3. McIlroy, G., and C. Storbeck. "Development of Deaf Identity: An Ethnographic Study." *Journal of Deaf Studies and Deaf Education, 16,* no. 4 (2011): pp. 497-98.
4. Charlton, James I. *Nothing About Us Without Us: Disability Oppression and Empowerment.* Berkeley: University of California Press, 1998, pp. 3-18.
5. "What Is Universal Design." Centre for Excellence in Universal Design. Accessed November 9, 2023. https://universaldesign.ie/What-is-Universal-Design/.
6. Mather, Susan M., and M. Diane Clark. "An Issue of Learning the Effect of Visual Split Attention in Classes for Deaf and Hard of Hearing Students." Odyssey, 2012, pp. 20-24
7. *YouTube.* YouTube. Accessed November 9, 2023. https://www.youtube.com/playlist?list=PL8oMa2koHkSJWCxWxqdCFTf_yd7acCv4T.
8. "The Vlog Project." Whitney Museum of American Art. Accessed November 9, 2023. https://whitney.org/education/access/vlogs.
9. Morris, Karla Kmetz, Casey Frechette, Lyman Dukes, Nicole Stowell, Emert Topping, and David Brodosi. "Closed Captioning Matters: Examining the Value of Closed Captions for All Students." *Journal of Postsecondary Education and Disability* 29, no. 3 (n.d.): 231-38.
10. "The ASL App." The ASL App. Accessed November 9, 2023. https://theaslapp.com/.
11. Andrews, J. O., S. D. Newman, O. Meadows, M. J. Cox, and S. Bunting. "Partnership Readiness for Community-Based Participatory Research." *Health Education Research* 27, no. 4 (2010): 555-71. https://doi.org/10.1093/her/cyq050.
12. "DE'VIA." MDHAC. Accessed November 9, 2023. https://www.museumofdeaf.org/de-via.
13. Frechtling, Joy A., and Henry T. Frierson. "Strategies That Address Culturally Responsive Evaluation." *The 2002 User Friendly Handbook of Project Evaluation*, National Science Foundation, Directorate for Education & Human Resources, Division of Research, Evaluation and Communication, Arlington, VA, 2002, pp. 63-72.

BIBLIOGRAPHY

Andrews, J. O., S. D. Newman, O. Meadows, M. J. Cox, and S. Bunting. "Partnership Readiness for Community-Based Participatory Research." *Health Education Research* 27, no. 4 (2010): 555-71. https://doi.org/10.1093/her/cyq050.

The ASL App. "The ASL App." Accessed November 9, 2023. https://theaslapp.com/.

Charlton, James I. *Nothing About Us Without Us: Disability Oppression and Empowerment.* Berkeley: University of California Press, 1998, pp. 3-18.

Frechtling, Joy A., and Henry T. Frierson. "Strategies That Address Culturally Responsive Evaluation." *The 2002 User Friendly Handbook of Project Evaluation*, National Science Foundation, Directorate for Education & Human Resources, Division of Research, Evaluation and Communication, Arlington, VA, 2002, pp. 63-72.

Lynch, Bernadette T. Custom-made Reflective Practice: Can Museums Realise Their Capabilities in Helping Others Realise Theirs?, *Museum Management and Curatorship*, 26, no. 5 (2011): 441-58, doi: 10.1080/09647775.2011.621731, pp. 441-58.

Mather, Susan M., and M. Diane Clark. "An Issue of Learning the Effect of Visual Split Attention in Classes for Deaf and Hard of Hearing Students." *Odyssey* (2012) pp. 20-24.

McIlroy, G., & Storbeck, C. Development of Deaf Identity: An Ethnographic Study. *Journal of Deaf Studies and Deaf Education, 16*, no. 4 (2011): 494–511. doi:10.1093/deafed /enr017.

MDHAC "DE'VIA.". Accessed November 9, 2023. https://www.museumofdeaf.org /de-via.

Morris, Karla Kmetz, Casey Frechette, Lyman Dukes, Nicole Stowell, Emert Topping, and David Brodosi. "Closed Captioning Matters: Examining the Value of Closed Captions for All Students." *Journal of Postsecondary Education and Disability* 29, no. 3 (n.d.): 231–38.

"Real-Time Captioning (CART)." Deaf and Hard of Hearing, August 30, 2022. https:// mn.gov/deaf-hard-of-hearing/communication-access/cart/.

"What Is Universal Design." Centre for Excellence in Universal Design. Accessed November 9, 2023. https://universaldesign.ie/What-is-Universal-Design/.

Whitney Museum of American Art. "The Vlog Project." Accessed November 9, 2023. https://whitney.org/education/access/vlogs.

YouTube. *YouTube.* Accessed November 9, 2023. https://www.youtube.com/play list?list=PL8oMa2koHkSJWCxWxqdCFTf_yd7acCv4T

Index

Page references for figures are italicized.

About the Editor

Laureen Trainer (she/her) is founder and principal of Trainer Evaluation in Denver, Colorado. She is passionate about evaluation as a tool for growth, adaptation, and engaging internal stakeholders and community members. Trainer began her career as a museum educator, switching to museum evaluation when she saw the need for understanding impact and identifying opportunities for learning and change. She worked as an internal evaluator at the Denver Museum of Nature and Science for several years before founding Trainer Evaluation to work for, and in collaboration with, small to midsize cultural- and informal-learning institutions.

As former editor of the blog for the Committee an Audience Research and Evaluation, a Professional Network of the American Alliance of Museums, Trainer curated nineteen blogs and worked with dozens of authors from the museum field. She coedited a volume of the *Journal of Museum Education* (JME), *Empowering Museum Educators to Evaluate* (Volume 40:1, 2015), coauthored the upcoming article, "Who's in Charge Here? Evaluating the Impacts of Sharing Authority with Children," and has been a JME peer reviewer for over a decade. Trainer holds a MA in art history and an MS in museum studies and is actively involved in the Colorado Evaluation Network and the Denver Evaluation Network.

About the Contributors

Dillyn Adamo (she/they) graduated from University of Washington's MA museology degree with a specialization in museum evaluation, where they focused on accessibility and interdisciplinary learning in museums. Dillyn currently serves as the learning and engagement coordinator at the Museum of Northwest Art.

Malikai Bass (he/him) first discovered his passion for addressing accessibility barriers in cultural learning institutions through personal experiences as a disabled child and teen involved in museum programming. He believes evaluation is an important tool for holding museums accountable to fulfilling their potential and promise for providing equitable access to ideas, knowledge, and belonging when other institutions fall short. While pursuing his master's degree in museology and specialization in museum evaluation at the University of Washington, he was able to implement several studies focusing on identifying and removing barriers to access.

Karen Breece (she/her) is the audience research and evaluation associate at Conner Prairie. In her role, she oversees twenty to thirty evaluation projects annually and is proud to work in a museum setting that constantly calls her to use innovative data collection methods. She brings her practical museum know-how gained through roles in museum education, public programs, and exhibit curation to her evaluation work, and strives to center the joy and well-being of museum visitors in everything she does. She has presented her work at the preeminent conference for museum evaluation professionals, the conference of the Visitor Studies Association. She holds a master's degree in museum studies from Indiana University.

Sarah Brenkert (she/her) is the principal evaluator at the Seattle Aquarium in Seattle, Washington, and serves as the faculty lead for the evaluation specialization in the University of Washington's master of arts in museology program. Sarah has a background in informal learning theory, exhibit design and development, and early childhood education. Sarah previously worked in education and evaluation at Denver Zoo and spent ten years as the senior director of education and evaluation at the Children's Museum of Denver in Denver, Colorado. Sarah graduated from Carleton College with a bachelor of arts and holds a master of science degree in early childhood and elementary education from Bank Street College of Education in New York City.

Alyssa Carr (she/her) specializes in visitor research and evaluation in her role as evaluation and visitor research associate at the Nelson-Atkins Museum of Art in Kansas City, Missouri. She prioritizes community engagement and participatory analysis of accessibility and IDEAs-centered projects. She has presented on participatory evaluation, evaluation of accessibility projects, and audience research. She is the current chair of the visitor studies association art museum focused interest group. Previous focus areas have included early education, military leadership, and youth and adult education. She holds a master's degree in organizational development from Avila University in Kansas City, Missouri.

Lisa Eriksen is an independent consultant who assists museums and cultural organizations by providing innovative foresight training, strategic planning, fundraising, and program services with a focus on planning for a preferred future. From 2018 to 2022, Lisa served as the accessibility coordinator at the Palo Alto Museum & Zoo, where she managed an Institute of Museum and Library Services–funded project to make the new facility and exhibitions accessible to visitors with disabilities. Lisa holds a certificate in strategic foresight from the University of Houston, served on faculty at the John F. Kennedy University museum studies program, and as a board member of the American Association for State and Local History and Western Museums Association. She is currently serving on the board of San Felipe Supported Living, an organization supporting individuals with developmental disabilities who are living in their own homes in a manner that recognizes the dignity and uniqueness of each person.

Tina Keegan is the exhibits director at the Palo Alto Junior Museum & Zoo in California. She has worked in various science and children's museums since 1998 and has an industrial design degree from Rhode Island School of Design. At the Junior Museum & Zoo, she was the project director for the IMLS-funded project, Access from the Ground Up. The ambitious project created accessible features throughout the newly rebuilt facility and embedded access and inclusion in all business practices. She started the museum's accessibility initiative in 2009 and has nurtured it since then. Throughout the IMLS project, she and the accessibility coordinator implemented design solutions to complex access problems with input from an accessibility advisory team. Throughout her career, Tina has been dedicated to accessible exhibit design but has learned that one department in a museum cannot solve access issues, and inclusion must be a comprehensive approach.

Lynda Kennedy, PhD, serves as the Intrepid Museum's vice president of education and evaluation, heading a department that includes the museum's access team. A career of thirty years includes positions integrating education, community engagement, and accessibility at institutions such as the Lower East Side Tenement Museum, the Museum of the Moving Image, and the New York Public Library, along with adjunct faculty appointments to the master of science in education programs of Hunter College and Metropolitan College of New York. She is a former Chair of the NYC Museum Educators Roundtable, past president of the International Museum Theater Alliance and served as a national associate for the American Alliance of Museum's Committee on Education. Dr. Kennedy holds a PhD in urban education from the Graduate Center of the City University of New York. Her research interests center on using resources of cultural institutions to support student engagement and teacher growth, arts integration across the disciplines, and decreasing the opportunity gap for students of all backgrounds and abilities.

Ellie Kravets (she/her) currently serves as the community programs coordinator for the Friends of the Anacortes Community Forest Lands. She holds a master of arts in museology from the University of Washington with a specialization in museum evaluation. Her work focuses on the role(s) that small science centers play in their communities, including how those organizations can leverage their networks to provide equitable access to their work. Ellie previously served as an educator in various capacities at the Port Townsend Marine Science Center in Port Townsend, Washington, and at the Dunes Learning Center in Porter, Indiana, and holds a bachelor of science in biology from the University of North Carolina at Chapel Hill.

Elizabeth Kunz Kollmann is the director of the research and evaluation department at the Museum of Science, Boston (MOS). In that role, Ms. Kollmann oversees a team of ten researchers and evaluators who study a range of informal STEM education experiences from in-museum exhibits and programs to out-of-school programs and professional development opportunities. A key focus of MOS evaluation work is helping teams to integrate universal design and universal design for learning principles and refine this work through audience feedback to improve accessibility. Ms. Kollmann holds a master of liberal arts in museum studies from the Harvard University Extension School.

Charlotte J. Martin (she/her) has fifteen years of experience working in museum education and accessibility. She is director of access initiatives at the Intrepid Museum, where she and her team develop specialized programs and resources and collaborate across the institution to embed accessibility in programming, training, customer service, design, infrastructure, and hiring. Charlotte has presented at conferences around the world and worked and consulted at a variety of museums. She previously served as president of the NYC Museum Educators Roundtable. Charlotte has an MAT in museum education from George Washington University and a BA in history of art from Yale University.

Leigh Ann Mesiti Caulfield is a senior experience researcher at BORN XDS. In this role, she helps clients make data-informed and human-centered decisions about the products, services, and systems they develop through discovery and user experience research. She co-leads the agency's accessibility initiative, which is a cross-agency, cross-disciplinary team that works towards strengthening and promoting accessibility capabilities and supports new and ongoing accessibility-related client work. Prior to BORN XDS, Leigh Ann spent over a decade at the Museum of Science, Boston, collaborating with in-house teams to design and prototype new experiences. Her role on these projects, and many others, involved a commitment to improving the accessibility of public spaces, exhibits, and programming for all visitors, including people with disabilities. Leigh Ann holds a BA in art history from Simmons College and an MEd in curriculum and instruction from Boston College. She is also an IAAP CPACC–Certified Professional in accessibility core competencies.

Tim Porter is senior director of public science communication at the Museum of Science, Boston, where he oversees the exhibits, programs, project management, community engagement, live animal center, collections, and archives teams. In his three decades of experience in museum education and administration, first at Boston Children's Museum and then the Museum of Science, Mr. Porter has spearheaded the creation of exhibits, programs, curricula, teacher professional development, and digital products that have reached tens of millions of people across the country and around the world. He has served as principal investigator (PI) and co-PI on National Science Foundation, Institute of Museum & Library Services, and NASA grants, and several state and foundation-funded exhibits, websites, and informal education programs.

Heather Pressman (she/her) is an educator with a passion for accessibility and inclusion. She believes that everyone has the right to access and enjoy cultural experiences regardless of their abilities or disabilities. Heather currently serves as the director of learning and engagement for the Molly Brown House Museum where she works to expand access, despite the physical challenges of a more than 130-year-old historic house. She got into this work because she saw through her friend's experience how much people with disabilities were missing out on in museums and at historic sites. Heather holds a master's degree in museum studies from Johns Hopkins University where she teaches accessibility in the museum. She coauthored *The Art of Access: A Practical Guide for Museum Accessibility* (Rowman & Littlefield, 2021) and is the editor of *An Accessible Past: Making Historic Sites Access* (Rowman & Littlefield, 2023).

Sarah Schleuning is dedicated to presenting and promoting the power and impact of art, architecture, and design to the public through exhibitions, publications, and programming. Currently the Margot B. Perot Senior Curator of Decorative Arts and Design at the Dallas Museum of Art, Schleuning has a record of organizing thoughtful exhibitions and programs that are not only high profile and highly popular, but also recognized for their contributions to scholarship. With her groundbreaking project, *speechless: different by design*, Schleuning built on her work with interactive public playscapes and accessibility. She has continued the work to pioneer ways museums can be more inclusive to our colleagues and communities. Prior to Dallas, she has held curatorial positions at the High Museum of Art, the Wolfsonian–Florida International University, and Cranbrook Art Museum. Schleuning graduated from Cornell University College of Arts and Sciences with a bachelor of arts. She received her master of arts in the history of decorative arts from Cooper-Hewitt National Design Museum in conjunction with Parsons School of Design. She frequently contributes to scholarly publications and serves as a leading resource for decorative arts and design, delivering lectures and speaking at symposiums and public programs throughout the country.

Danielle Schulz (she/her) is dedicated to an accessible and inclusive future. She currently serves as the associate director of lifelong learning and accessibility at the Denver Art Museum, where she works with colleagues and community members to promote inclusive practices, programs, and trainings that ensure visitors of all ages and abilities can enjoy and be inspired by their interaction with art, and that museum staff and volunteers are empowered to welcome people with disabilities into museum spaces. She coauthored *The Art of Access: A Practical Guide for Museum Accessibility* (Rowman & Littlefield, 2021) and received a master's degree in art education from the University of Texas at Austin.

Maia Swinson (she/her) served as an audience research and evaluation intern at Conner Prairie in the summer of 2023. New to the field of museum evaluation, she spent her internship evaluating Conner Prairie's programs while researching the connection between health and museum attendance. Maia is passionate about museum and community-based groups partnering with public health organizations to aid in improving human wellbeing. Prior to coming to Conner Prairie, she assisted in research and evaluation for nonprofits in the Chicago area. Maia recently graduated from Wheaton College with a bachelor's of science in applied health science and a public health certificate.

Kelsey Van Voorst (they/she) is currently the education operations manager at the Indianapolis Zoo. Previously, they had been in management at Conner Prairie architecting and producing programs throughout the year specifically designed for individuals with visible and invisible differences and abilities. Kelsey has over thirteen years of experience in a variety of museums, zoos, aquariums, and botanical gardens around the United States. Kelsey also serves as a board member for two small visual and performing arts nonprofits based in central Indiana. Kelsey holds an MPA in nonprofit management from Indiana University, Indianapolis.

Maia Werner-Avidon, principal of MWA Insights, is an established independent evaluator working with museums and other cultural institutions. Prior to starting her firm, Ms. Werner-Avidon served as the manager of research and evaluation for the Asian Art Museum in San Francisco and as a research and evaluation specialist at the Lawrence Hall of Science (Berkeley, California). She earned her bachelor's degree from Macalester College and master of arts degree in museum studies from John F. Kennedy University. Ms. Werner-Avidon served as the external evaluator for the Access from the Ground Up project at the Palo Alto Junior Museum & Zoo.